THE
ENGLISH
LIBRARY

General Editor JAMES SUTHERLAND
*Emeritus Professor of Modern Literature
University College, London*

Selected Poems of
SAMUEL JOHNSON
and
OLIVER GOLDSMITH

Edited by ALAN RUDRUM
Lecturer in English, The Queen's University, Belfast
and PETER DIXON
Lecturer in English, Queen Mary College, London

UNIVERSITY OF SOUTH CAROLINA PRESS
Columbia, S.C.

© A. Rudrum and P. Dixon 1965

Published 1965 in Great Britain by
EDWARD ARNOLD (PUBLISHERS) LTD.
41 Maddox Street, London W.1

Published 1970 in the United States of America by the
UNIVERSITY OF SOUTH CAROLINA PRESS
Columbia, S.C. 29208

Standard Book Number: 87249-151-x
Library of Congress Catalog Card Number: 76-116468

Manufactured in Great Britain

General Preface

THE design of this series is to present fully annotated selections from English literature which will, it is hoped, prove satisfactory both in their breadth and their depth. To achieve this some of the volumes have been planned so as to provide a varied selection from the poetry or prose of a limited period, which is at once long enough to have developed a literary movement and short enough to allow for adequate representation of the chief writers and of the various crosscurrents within the movement. Examples of such periods are the late seventeenth century and the early eighteenth century. In other volumes the principle of selection is to present a literary kind (e.g. satirical poetry, the literary ballad). Here it is possible to cover a longer period without sacrificing the unified and comprehensive treatment which is the governing idea for the whole series. Other volumes, again, are designed to present a group of writers who form some kind of "school" (e.g. the Elizabethan sonneteers, the followers of Ben Jonson), or who were closely enough linked for their work to be brought together (e.g. the poetry of Johnson and Goldsmith).

Each volume has a full critical introduction. Headnotes, a special feature of this series, provide relevant background and critical comment for the individual poems and prose pieces. The footnotes are for the most part explanatory, giving as briefly as possible information about persons, places, allusions of one kind or another, the meaning of words, etc., which the twentieth-century reader is likely to require. Each selection aims at providing examples of the best work of the authors represented, but it is hoped that the inclusion of some less familiar pieces not available in any other collection will widen the reader's experience and enjoyment of the literature under review. The series is intended for use in universities and the upper forms of schools.

For the study of English neoclassical poetry the work of Samuel Johnson and Oliver Goldsmith provides an excellent point of departure. Different though those two poets were in character and temperament, their poetry is marked by the same determination to "survey mankind, from China to Peru", and to see human life with the eyes of the moralist whose judgements are founded on personal experience and reflect a serious concern for the lot of mankind on earth. If Johnson's outlook is sombre, and Goldsmith's is touched with a nostalgic sadness for happier times, both men looked at life steadily and gave a true report of what they found. In their minor poems (more especially those of Goldsmith) the tone is often lighter, but the thought and expression remain impeccably precise and controlled. Although this edition of the poems of Johnson and Goldsmith does not present their complete poetical works, it offers a comprehensive selection which leaves out little that is of lasting value.

Selected Poems of
SAMUEL JOHNSON

edited by ALAN RUDRUM

Bibliographical Note

THE text used in this selection is that of the *Poems*, ed. D. Nichol Smith and E. L. McAdam, Oxford, 1941. We wish to thank the Clarendon Press for permission to reproduce the text and to draw upon some of the notes of that edition.

In the notes to this selection, *Life* refers to Boswell's *Life of Samuel Johnson*, ed. G. B. Hill, 6 vols., Oxford, 1887; revised L. F. Powell, 1934-50. *Dictionary* refers to Johnson's *Dictionary of the English Language*, which was first published in 1755.

For a guide to criticism of Johnson's poems the reader should consult J. L. Clifford, *Johnsonian Studies, 1887-1950*, University of Minnesota, 1951, pp. 93-5; and J. L. Clifford and D. J. Greene, "A Bibliography of Johnsonian Studies, 1950-1960," in *Johnsonian Studies*, ed. Magdi Wahba, Cairo, 1962. There is a short general bibliography in *The Pelican Guide to English Literature*, ed. B. Ford, vol. 4, pp. 481-2. On pp. 271-7 of that volume there is a reprint of a famous essay by T. S. Eliot, and on pp. 399-419 a useful essay by A. R. Humphreys. Ian Jack has an excellent chapter on *Vanity* in his *Augustan Satire*, Oxford, 1952, reprinted with corrections 1957. The reader should also see the chapter on Johnson in D. Nichol Smith, *Some Observations on Eighteenth-Century Poetry*, London, 1937; two essays by F. R. Leavis in *The Common Pursuit*, London, 1952, reprinted by Peregrine Books, 1962; and the chapter "The Augustan Tradition" in Dr. Leavis's *Revaluation*, London, 1953.

A very readable introduction to Juvenal is G. Highet, *Juvenal the Satirist*, Oxford, 1954. The article on Juvenal in the eleventh edition of the *Encyclopaedia Britannica* is also useful.

Contents

INTRODUCTION	10
CHRONOLOGICAL TABLE	18
Translation of Horace	19
Upon the Feast of St. Simon and St. Jude	20
London	23
An Epitaph on Claudy Phillips, a Musician	33
An Ode on Friendship	34
To Miss ——	35
Epitaph on Sir Thomas Hanmer	35
The Drury-Lane Prologue	37
The Vanity of Human Wishes	40
A New Prologue . . .	54
Translations from Boethius	55
Prologue to 'The Good Natur'd Man'	57
Epitaph on Hogarth	58
A Short Song of Congratulation	59
On the Death of Dr. Robert Levet	60

Introduction

JOHNSON'S poems deserve to be much more widely known. They are the work of the most important English writer between Pope and the Romantics, they illustrate certain basic virtues which our own poetry too frequently lacks, and they are very good poems. The fact that they are not more widely read is easily explained. Johnson as a poet has been overshadowed by Dryden and Pope, and, no doubt, by his own fame as a prose-writer; unfortunately few people become acquainted with *London* and *The Vanity of Human Wishes* during their school-days.

In our own time, when so many poets have devoted themselves to elaborating the nuances of the inexpressible, it is not surprising that we should be tempted to think of Johnson as lacking in some ingredient essential to poetry. Some good as well as much bad poetry has resulted from writers using language at a considerable remove from normal syntax and meaning—in a word, from eccentricity. Johnson claimed no such bardic privileges; not least among his aims was that his work should be understood by any normally well-educated man who cared to read it.

The notes on the poems which follow are intended to remove the obstacle of ignorance about the subjects of Johnson's allusions. A more serious barrier to appreciation is the common preconception that the poems consist mainly of inordinately dull and pompous moralisings, remote from the real interests of most readers. This is a belief which a first uncritical reading, particularly of *The Vanity of Human Wishes*, is likely to fix rather than to dispel. Perseverance will teach that in reality Johnson is as powerful and decisive in thought as he is subtle in versification.

The praise conventionally accorded to Johnson fails to do justice to those qualities which need to be stressed. Seriousness, dignity, weight, are qualities which he undoubtedly displays; but the stress ought equally to be laid on his unfailing vitality, his wit, his metrical control and the trenchancy of his diction—all of which we may miss if we approach him paralysed with the apprehension of boredom. Consider the description of the Frenchman from *London*, "Obsequious, artful, voluble and gay", or of the dotard from *Vanity*, "Perversely grave, or positively wrong", or, from the *coda* of *Vanity*, the line, "The secret ambush of a specious pray'r". These lines, like almost any others that one might choose, illustrate Johnson's artistic integrity; there are no verbal pyrotechnics for their own sake: the sound is perfectly adjusted to the meaning. And though it is true that examples of fine lines can be multiplied, one cannot in fact capture the full beauty of Johnson's music by isolated quotation. He has to a high degree the power to orchestrate a long passage; look, for example, at the famous episode in *Vanity* of Charles XII of Sweden, with its demonstrational rising and falling curve and its superbly prepared and executed conclusion. It is in the long verse-paragraph that we feel the vitality of Johnson's mind, not pushing mechanically along a prescribed course but sensitive in every line to the implications of the argument; here too that we realise, if we are sensible, how false is the old charge that Johnson had no ear for the music of verse. Like his great contemporary Gibbon, Johnson habitually composed whole paragraphs in his mind before putting pen to paper, with the result that his paragraphs have an organic unity and escape the weakness common in lesser authors of being simply a bundle of sentences held loosely together. Compare Johnson in this respect with his contemporary Edward Young, author of the *Night Thoughts*. Many of Young's lines have become proverbial, for example "Procrastination is the thief of time", and "A fool at forty is a fool indeed"; but Young's most successful lines invariably gain in force by being removed from their context, whereas in quoting Johnson one feels that the context is always implicated in the success of any individual line. When one gets to know *Vanity* well, one begins to feel that almost every line is somehow charged with the meaning of the whole poem. This is a tribute to the success with which Johnson is able to subdue his end-stopped couplets to an overall harmony, and to the moral passion which informs his work and prevents any part of it from being merely— or even mainly—decoration.

The most immediately relevant comparison is with Dryden's translation of the same satire of Juvenal; and this is a comparison which students are advised to make, in detail, for themselves. Most readers find Dryden's work the more attractive on a first reading, but closer acquaintance frequently reverses the estimate. Dryden's version is the more rapid; but Johnson's is equally vigorous, and more controlled. Dryden has passages which have more apparent vivacity, more obvious and immediate appeal, than anything in Johnson, but Johnson is more impressive in the mass— we can apprehend his work as a firm, coherent edifice. Dryden's most striking passages are those in which he recaptures an Elizabethan or Jacobean tang; Johnson's style is consistent throughout, in a manner which is so unobtrusive as to be unexciting until we pause to consider it. Johnson summed up Dryden's translation without malice but with complete accuracy when he remarked that "The general character of this translation will be given when it is said to preserve the wit, but to want the dignity of the original." Dryden refers to Juvenal's tenth as "this divine Satire", but it is Johnson's version which is the better sermon. Indeed, in this respect the protests of some readers are revealing: "It's too pessimistic" is a frequent charge, and such a comment is symptomatic of the salutary uneasiness which the poem is apt to produce in the careful reader; we can feel it tugging at our emotions, seeking to modify our unthinking optimisms, insistently requiring the admission that human existence is indeed like this and not what in our daily lives we implicitly make of it. However, the charge of pessimism needs to be modified. It is true, as Ian Jack has said, that the rhetorical tone throughout *Vanity* is designed to "diminish" human life; but Johnson's concern, as he ranges through "every state" of humankind, is directed towards his final question, which has more than rhetorical force: "Where then shall Hope and Fear their objects find?" With the weight of the poem behind it, the conclusion stands for more than mere solace: it blends our perceptions into a genuine insight into the nature of human existence. Implicit throughout is the traditional Christian insistence that we must control our desires and sanctify our passions; whether the sermon has lost its relevance, introspection and observation may decide.

Johnson's ability to *sound* interesting has already been noticed. The subtlety of his writing is suggested by the very simplicity of his rhetorical devices, to explain which, one feels, is by no means to explain the effects which Johnson obtains with them. One such device is the sort of witty juxtaposition in which Pope excelled. An example from *Vanity* is the conclusion of the passage on Archbishop Laud:

> Around his tomb let Art and Genius weep,
> But hear his death, ye blockheads, hear and sleep.

Here effect is gained by the juxtaposition of the lofty abstractions "Art" and "Genius" with the contemptuously familiar "blockheads". Part of the strength of the passage derives from the contrast of the Latin with the Teutonic elements in the language. Johnson's sensitivity to this aspect of composition had no doubt been sharpened by his work on the *Dictionary*, and it is responsible for some of his happiest touches. One recalls the lines in the poem on the death of Dr. Robert Levet, who is described as

> Officious, innocent, sincere,
> Of ev'ry friendless name the friend.

Here the Latinate undertones of each word in the first line, contrasting with the Teutonic elements of the second, magnetise the reader's attention.

Another example of verbal wit, this time from *London*, is in the condemnation of such flatterers as

> Exalt each trifle, ev'ry vice adore,
> Your taste in snuff, your judgment in a whore.

Here the witty collocation of the lofty "judgment" with the low "whore" condemns flatterer and flattered alike. It ironically points up the futility of bringing "judgment" to bear upon such matters (is it too fanciful to suppose that the idea of the Supreme Judge and the Day of Judgment influenced Johnson's choice of word?); it suggests also condemnation of the attitude towards the whore, who is *used* in a way which degrades her and her client alike, reduced to the level of horseflesh, to be "judged" according to her "points". Effective too is the rhyming, which sets the heights of romantic and religious devotion against the depths of human degradation: "adore" and "a whore", sounding so alike, meaning so differently, interact to enforce our recognition of the moral tragedy ensuing upon frivolous choices. The critic, to indicate these things even superficially, must employ an awkward longhand; in the poem moral emerges from verbal wit with immediate impact: the point is made memorably and with great economy.

Both T. S. Eliot and Dr. Leavis have pointed out that Johnson's demonstrations are not of the dramatic kind: we do not find in *Vanity* what we find in *Lear* or *Women in Love*, the discovery and testing of moral principles in the very heart of experience. Johnson's judgments do not have that peculiar authority which stems from the reader's participation in their dramatic enaction. Nor perhaps is it necessary that they should, since he deals in truths of which all need to be reminded, but few informed: he is a conservative moralist, examining old truths in the light of his own experience, rather than a spiritual spearhead of humanity like Blake or Lawrence. However, while conceding the point made by Eliot and Leavis, it must be said that of course Johnson offers us more than a mere simple statement of moral principles. There is nearly always, in *Vanity*, a realising quality, as in the last lines quoted, where the wit renders the moral unarguable, or as in what has already been referred to as the demonstrational rising and falling curve in the Charles XII of Sweden passage. This is to say that Johnson's moralising does possess the authority conferred by art; it is arguable that *Vanity* enforces its central proposition more finely than *Ecclesiastes*, which in a sense ranks equally with Juvenal's tenth satire as the original of Johnson's poem.

Juvenal was a skilful rhetorician, probably a legal advocate, for many years before he wrote his satires, and one of the elements that Johnson admired in them, and sought to transfer to his imitations, was their rhetorical excellence. He does in fact very successfully imitate Juvenal's persuasive force. One of his techniques is the simple use of repetition; look, for example, at the "poverty" passage in *London* and, in *Vanity*, at the episodes of the scholar and of Charles of Sweden. In these passages, the effect of the repetition, combined as it is with Johnson's metrical firmness, is to project a controlled vehemence, a passion that convinces of its validity because it does not alienate the reader by incoherence or overstatement. Johnson's metrical skill deserves more than passing notice: his versification establishes his authority. It is significant that the words which describe it, strength, vivacity, control and wit, are also applicable to moral and intellectual qualities that call forth trust and admiration. His diction may be described in similar terms; it is language used very differently from that of Shakespeare or Donne, but if it is the common language of prose discourse, it is that language used with great economy and relevance, once again qualities we associate with moral and intellectual integrity. Take these two lines from "The Ant", which is not a particularly good poem, and is not printed in this selection:

> How long shall sloth usurp thy useless hours,
> Dissolve thy vigour, and enchain thy powers?

Here we see that the metaphors "dissolve" and "enchain" offer no shock of surprise to the reader; the interesting thing is that they are not oppressively *cliché*. They are saved partly by Johnson's metrical skill: they are placed very firmly, whereas *cliché* normally floats uneasily in a stew of sloppiness. They are also saved by Johnson's precision: he is not in the least afraid to use commonplace words, but he does so with a quite uncommon regard for their meanings. Sometimes this combination of metrical control and semantic awareness calls forth surprising intensities from the simplest materials, as in the final stanza of "On the Death of Dr. Robert Levet":

> Then with no throbbing fiery pain,
>   No cold gradations of decay,
> Death broke at once the vital chain,
>   And free'd his soul the nearest way.

One reason perhaps why we do not take easily to Johnson is that some modern novelists have accustomed us to extremely minute analysis of particular psychological states. In his essay, "Surgery for the Novel—Or a Bomb", D. H. Lawrence has vigorously deprecated this "picking of self-consciousness into small bits"; perhaps more to our purpose is the consideration that we should guard against condemning Johnson for not doing what he did not want to do. It is worth while to recall Imlac's dissertation on poetry from the tenth chapter of *Rasselas*: "The business of a poet is to examine, not the individual, but the species; to remark general properties and large appearances . . . he must . . . rise to general and transcendental truths, which will always be the same." In the same vein there is Johnson's remark in the *Preface to Shakespeare* that "Nothing can please many, and please long, but just representations of general nature." To return to the lines quoted above from "The Ant", we should not blame Johnson because he does not render the *nuances* of a particular individual bondage to sloth; it is important not to mistake for vagueness Johnson's addiction to the word which expresses the common factor, the generally important element, in any psychological situation.

Any account of Johnson's technique should seek to answer the question of how it is that he is able to use abstractions and generalisations so successfully. The technical devices to which one can point are so simple that the pointing must appear to beg the question, but the fact is that Johnson is more elusive of full critical description than many apparently more subtle poets.

One device aimed at achieving a high generality has been pointed out by Ian Jack, who in *Augustan Satire* notices that Johnson makes frequent use of the combination "the" plus generalised adjective plus generalised noun, as in "the toiling statesman", "the needy traveller", "the glittering eminence". Nothing could be simpler, and the surprising thing is that we are convinced of the representative quality of the figures Johnson thus sets up. Here as elsewhere we see Johnson's ability to seize on the essential elements in any situation: the *justness* of his language is what impresses as we come to know his poems better:

> See nations slowly wise, and meanly just,
> To buried merit raise the tardy bust.

Lines such as these call for the reader to be wide awake; the wit, the relevance, the economy are then seen to serve a moral passion, a meaning which is personally experienced though impersonally expressed. Similarly, what could be more just than the train of adjectives in

> His fall was destin'd to a barren strand,
> A petty fortress, and a dubious hand.

Taken in context, these quiet adjectives become charged with the force of a tragedy which is both personal and representative.

Sometimes validity is achieved by Johnson's easy movement between the large generality and the illuminating particular. See, for instance, the sharp focusing of his general theme in the passage on the horrors of old age from *Vanity*:

> From Lydia's monarch should the search descend,
> By Solon caution'd to regard his end,
> In life's last scene what prodigies surprise,
> Fears of the brave, and follies of the wise?
> From Marlb'rough's eyes the streams of dotage flow,
> And Swift expires a driv'ler and a show.

Usually, however, Johnson relies on the reader's sense of the truthfulness of his generalisations; and in practice the more we know, the more freely we assent, whether Johnson is dealing with intellectual matters or the truths of moral experience. Consider, for example, Johnson's account of the decline of tragic drama in the Restoration period and during the eighteenth century:

> Then crush'd by Rules, and weaken'd as refin'd,
> For Years the Pow'r of Tragedy declin'd;
> From Bard, to Bard, the frigid Caution crept,
> Till Declamation roar'd, while Passion slept.

No summary could be more true to particular instances, more generally applicable, than that last line. All this implies that Johnson requires his readers to have some interest in the matters about which he writes, at a level more fundamental than the slickness of coffee-bar intellectualism. As he wrote himself, he was "by wit, by knowledge, studious to be read". Every such reader must necessarily be one who has attempted, in the interests of the intellectual life, to insulate himself against the petty flurry of diurnal distractions; and any such will acknowledge at once the justness of Johnson's passage on the temptations which deflect scholars from their purposes. It is instructive to notice that this passage, which reflects Johnson's own experience more directly perhaps than any other in *Vanity*, is actually even more impersonal than most others in the poem. It is not that it is less emotional—Johnson's intellectualism is always highly charged with feeling—but that the emotion is depersonalised; to adapt T. S. Eliot's phrase, the man who suffers is never permitted, in Johnson, to interfere with the mind which creates.

Indeed, one's conclusion is that the very aspect of *Vanity* which tends to repel us initially, is what finally engages our admiration: its impersonality comes to be seen as an impressive literary and psychological achievement. It is only on a callow reading that we mistake absence of egotism for deficiency in human interest. The poems are free from the projection of Johnson's ego, and from indulgence in contemporary personalities. Johnson's practice was impressively consistent; his recorded conversation is singularly free from gossip, and in the last number of the *Rambler* he says rightly, "I have rarely exemplified my assertions by living characters", and "I have never complied with contemporary curiosity nor enabled my readers to discuss the topic of the day." There is no "human interest" in the debased modern sense about Johnson's portraits; if we examine the Wolsey episode in *Vanity* as an example, we find that the sketch, while vigorous and accurate, is highly generalised. "Law in his voice, and fortune in his hand" is representative in that, while it is true enough of Wolsey, its purpose is to symbolise the attributes of a condition of life rather than a particular person. Johnson's skill consists in picking out those details which are true of the particular case and have an additional representative quality: "The golden canopy, the glitt'ring plate,/The regal palace, the luxurious board." His practice is reflected in the entry under "Satire", in the *Dictionary*: "Proper satire is distinguished, by the generality of the reflections, from the lampoon."

Our main stress in these remarks has been on *Vanity*. There is no disagreeing with the opinion that here is Johnson's masterpiece; as Boswell put it, "as high an effort of ethick poetry as any language can show". There is no other poem like it in English. However, recognition of the great excellence of *Vanity* should not cause us to underestimate *London* and the shorter poems. This selection has been made in the conviction that Johnson wrote a larger number of good poems than is usually allowed. Whatever the subject, or the occasion, Johnson exhibits the same care and control in versification and diction, the same attention to overall structure, the same economy, relevance and adequacy of phrase, and, when treating of people, the same dignity, clarity of insight, and humane concern.

A. W. Rudrum

Chronological Table

1709 Born at Lichfield, September 18.
1728 Pembroke College, Oxford.
1729 Leaves Oxford.
1732 Usher at Market Bosworth School.
1735 Marries Mrs. Elizabeth Porter, and opens a school near Lichfield.
1737 Goes to London with one of his pupils, David Garrick. Returns to Lichfield where he finishes *Irene*. Settles in London.
1738 Writing for *The Gentleman's Magazine*. Publishes *London*.
1744 *Life of Mr. Richard Savage*.
1747 *Plan of a Dictionary of the English Language*.
1749 *The Vanity of Human Wishes*. *Irene* produced by Garrick, and published.
1750-2 *The Rambler*.
1752 Death of Johnson's wife.
1755 *A Dictionary of the English Language*.
1758-60 *The Idler*.
1759 Death of Johnson's mother. *Rasselas*.
1762 Receives Government pension.
1763 Meeting of Johnson and Boswell.
1765 Edition of Shakespeare.
1775 *A Journey to the Western Isles of Scotland*.
1779-81 *Lives of the Most Eminent English Poets*.
1783 Dies, December 13; buried in Westminster Abbey.
1791 Boswell's *Life of Samuel Johnson, LL.D.*

Translation of Horace

ODES, Book II, xiv

THIS poem was written when Johnson was fifteen, and published in full for the first time in *The Poems of Samuel Johnson*, ed. D. Nichol Smith and Edward L. McAdam, 1941.

>   Alass, dear Friend, the fleeting years
>   In everlasting Circles run,
>   In vain you spend your vows and prayers,
>   They roll, and ever will roll on.
>
> 5 Should Hecatombs each rising Morn
>   On cruel Pluto's Altar dye,
>   Should costly Loads of incense burn,
>   Their fumes ascending to the Skie;
>
>   You could not gain a Moments breath,
> 10 Or move the haughty King below,
>   Nor would inexorable Death
>   Defer an hour the fatal blow.
>
>   In vain we shun the Din of war,
>   And terrours of the Stormy Main,

    5 *Hecatombs:* Johnson's usage, referring to the sacrificial objects rather than to the sacrificial act, points back to the origins of the word (Greek: a hundred oxen). By the time of Homer the meaning had become generalised to indicate merely a great public sacrifice.

    6 Pluto, the Greek god of the lower world (the "haughty King below" of line 10), is unresponsive both to prayer and to sacrifice.

15 In vain with anxious breasts we fear
    Unwholesome Sirius' sultry reign;

    We all must view the Stygian flood
    That silent cuts the dreary plains,
    And cruel Danaus' bloody Brood
20 Condemn'd to everduring pains.

    Your shady Groves, your pleasing wife,
    And fruitfull fields, my dearest Friend,
    You'll leave together with your life,
    Alone the Cypress shall attend.

25 After your death, the lavish heir
    Will quickly drive away his woe,
    The wine you kept with so much care
    Along the marble floor shall flow.

16 *Sirius' sultry reign:* the hottest part of the year, associated with the heliacal rising of Sirius, the dog-star, and hence called the dog-days. Because this time of year brought pestilence, the Romans sacrificed dogs to placate the hostile star. Sirius, the brightest star in the heavens, is situated in the constellation *Canis Major*.

17 *Stygian flood:* the river Styx marks the boundary of the underworld.

19 Danaus had fifty daughters, forty-nine of whom, on Danaus' instructions, slew their husbands. Their punishment in the underworld was the endless task of filling with water a vessel which had no bottom.

24 The cypress tree, which never grows again when cut down, was a symbol of the dead, and sacred to Pluto.

Upon the Feast of St. Simon and St. Jude

THIS poem, probably written when Johnson was seventeen, was published for the first time by Nichol Smith and McAdam. It celebrates the tradition that these saints were martyred, Simon in Britain, Jude in Persia. It is Johnson's only poem in this stanza-form, which is that used by Christopher Smart, some thirty years later, in *A Song to David*.

UPON THE FEAST OF ST. SIMON AND ST. JUDE

    Of Fields with dead bestrew'd around,
    And Cities smoaking on the ground
        Let vulgar Poets sing,
    Let them prolong their turgid lays
5 With some victorious Heroe's praise
        Or weep some falling King.

    While I to nobler themes aspire,
    To nobler subjects tune my lyre;
        Those Saints my numbers grace
10 Who to their Lord were ever dear,
    To whom the church each rolling year
        Her solemn honours pays.

    In vain proud tyrants strove to shake
    Their faith, or force them to forsake
15   The Steps their Saviour trod;
    With breasts resolv'd, they follow'd still
    Obsequious to his heav'nly will
        Their master and their God.

    When Christ had conquer'd Hell and fate
20 And rais'd us from our wreched state,
        O prodigy of Love!
    Ascending to the skies he shone
    Refulgent on his starry throne
        Among the Saints above.

25 Th' Apostles round the world were sent,
    Dispersing blessings as they went,
        Thro' all the spacious ball;
    Far from their happy native home
    They, pleas'd, thro' barb'rous nations roam
30   To raise them from their fall.

17 *Obsequious:* obedient.

>   Where Atlas was believ'd to bear
>   The weight of ev'ry rolling sphere,
>   Where sev'nmouth'd Nilus roars,
>   Where the darkvisag'd Natives fry,
> 35   And scarce can breath th' infected sky,
>   But bless the Northern shoars,
>
>   Simon by gen'rous Zeal inspir'd,
>   With ardent love of virtue fir'd,
>   There trod the Lybian sands,
> 40   Though fierce Barbarians threatend death
>   And Serpents with their poys'nous breath
>   Infest the barren Lands.
>
>   Nor there confin'd his active Soul;
>   But where the Realms beneath the Pole
> 45   In clouds of Ign'rance mourn,
>   Thither with eager hast he runs
>   And visits Britain's hardy Sons
>   Ah! never to return!
>
>   Nor whilst she Simons acts persues
> 50   Art thou forgotten by the Muse,
>   Most venerable Jude!
>   Where Tigris beats his sounding shore
>   The haughty Persian in thy gore
>   His wrathfull sword imbru'd.
>
> 55   Thrice happy Saints—where do I rove?
>   Where doth extatick fury move
>   My rude unpolish'd song;
>   Mine unharmonious verse profanes
>   Those names which in immortal strains
> 60   Angelick choirs have sung.

31 *Atlas:* a mountain in Libya that was regarded as supporting the heavens.

London

A POEM IN IMITATION OF THE THIRD SATIRE OF JUVENAL

London was published in 1738. Like *The Vanity of Human Wishes* it belongs to a class of composition very popular at that time, the *imitation*. Johnson defined imitation as "A method of translating looser than paraphrase, in which modern examples and illustrations are used for ancient, or domestick for foreign". In his *Life of Pope* he wrote: "This mode of imitation, in which the ancients are familiarised by adapting their sentiments to modern topicks... was first practised in the reign of Charles the Second by Oldham and Rochester, at least I remember no instances more ancient. It is a kind of middle composition between translation and original design, which pleases when the thoughts are unexpectedly applicable and the parallels lucky. It seems to have been Pope's favourite amusement, for he has carried it further than any former poet."

  Tho' grief and fondness in my breast rebel,
  When injur'd THALES bids the town farewell,
  Yet still my calmer thoughts his choice commend,
  I praise the hermit, but regret the friend,
5 Resolved at length, from vice and LONDON far,
  To breathe in distant fields a purer air,
  And, fix'd on Cambria's solitary shore,
  Give to St. David one true Briton more.
   For who would leave, unbrib'd, Hibernia's land,
10 Or change the rocks of Scotland for the Strand?
  There none are swept by sudden fate away,
  But all whom hunger spares, with age decay:
  Here malice, rapine, accident, conspire,
  And now a rabble rages, now a fire;

2 THALES corresponds to Juvenal's Umbricius, who is disgusted with life in Rome. It is unlikely that Johnson had any particular contemporary in mind.

7 *Cambria:* Wales. See the note on line 47. **8** *St. David:* the patron saint of Wales. **9** *Hibernia:* Ireland.

15 Their ambush here relentless ruffians lay,
    And here the fell attorney prowls for prey;
    Here falling houses thunder on your head,
    And here a female atheist talks you dead.
       While THALES waits the wherry that contains
20 Of dissipated wealth the small remains,
    On Thames's banks, in silent thought we stood,
    Where Greenwich smiles upon the silver flood:
    Struck with the seat that gave Eliza birth,
    We kneel, and kiss the consecrated earth;
25 In pleasing dreams the blissful age renew,
    And call Britannia's glories back to view;
    Behold her cross triumphant on the main,
    The guard of commerce, and the dread of Spain,
    Ere masquerades debauch'd, excise oppress'd,
30 Or English honour grew a standing jest.
       A transient calm the happy scenes bestow,
    And for a moment lull the sense of woe.
    At length awaking, with contemptuous frown,
    Indignant THALES eyes the neighb'ring town.
35   Since worth, he cries, in these degen'rate days,
    Wants ev'n the cheap reward of empty praise;
    In those curs'd walls, devote to vice and gain,
    Since unrewarded science toils in vain;

17-18 Johnson follows Juvenal in mixing real and imaginary dangers.
19 *wherry:* "a light boat used on rivers" (*Dictionary*).
23 *Eliza:* Queen Elizabeth was born at Greenwich.
29 *excise:* "a hateful tax levied upon commodities" (*Dictionary*). The outcry against his excise proposals of 1733 marked a major setback for the Whig prime minister, Sir Robert Walpole. *London* was written when Walpole's power was in decline. Passages like this represent part of the then current flood of invective against Walpole.
30 Walpole's opponents wanted war with Spain, which claimed exclusive rights over the American continent and the right of searching English trading vessels. See line 54 and note.
35 The rest of the poem is a speech by Thales.
38 *science:* "any art or species of knowledge" (*Dictionary*).

Since hope but sooths to double my distress,
40 And ev'ry moment leaves my little less;
While yet my steady steps no staff sustains,
And life still vig'rous revels in my veins;
Grant me, kind heaven, to find some happier place,
Where honesty and sense are no disgrace;
45 Some pleasing bank where verdant osiers play,
Some peaceful vale with nature's paintings gay;
Where once the harrass'd Briton found repose,
And safe in poverty defy'd his foes;
Some secret cell, ye pow'rs, indulgent give.
50 Let —— live here, for —— has learn'd to live.
Here let those reign, whom pensions can incite
To vote a patriot black, a courtier white;
Explain their country's dear-bought rights away,
And plead for pirates in the face of day;
55 With slavish tenets taint our poison'd youth,
And lend a lye the confidence of truth.

 Let such raise palaces, and manors buy,
Collect a tax, or farm a lottery,

45 *osier:* "a tree of the willow kind" (*Dictionary*).

47 *the harrass'd Briton:* who retreated to Wales during the invasions by the Anglo-Saxons.

50 Johnson probably had no particular person in mind.

51 *pension:* "In England it is generally understood to mean pay given to a state hireling for treason to his country" (*Dictionary*).

52 The Tory opposition to Walpole were known as *patriots*; the Whigs were called *courtiers*, because of Walpole's influence over Queen Caroline.

54 "The invasions of the Spaniards were defended in the houses of Parliament" (Johnson). The "invasion" referred to is the searching of English trading vessels by the Spanish.

58 *farm a lottery:* "The government ... from 1709-1825, acted shamelessly in raising large sums annually by means of lotteries in which the prizes were terminable or perpetual annuities. Contractors took up the tickets and sent itinerant salesmen through the country, who sold fractions of the £10 shares.... In 1736 an act was passed for building Westminster Bridge by means of a lottery" (R. H. I. Palgrave, *Dictionary of Political Economy*, 1894).

With warbling eunuchs fill a licens'd stage,
60 And lull to servitude a thoughtless age.
    Heroes, proceed! what bounds your pride shall hold?
What check restrain your thirst of pow'r and gold?
Behold rebellious virtue quite o'erthrown,
Behold our fame, our wealth, our lives your own.
65   To such, a groaning nation's spoils are giv'n,
When publick crimes inflame the wrath of heav'n:
But what, my friend, what hope remains for me,
Who start at theft, and blush at perjury?
Who scarce forbear, tho' BRITAIN's Court he sing,
70 To pluck a titled Poet's borrow'd wing;
A Statesman's logick unconvinc'd can hear,
And dare to slumber o'er the Gazetteer;
Despise a fool in half his pension dress'd,
And strive in vain to laugh at H——y's jest.
75   Others with softer smiles, and subtler art,
Can sap the principles, or taint the heart;
With more address a lover's note convey,
Or bribe a virgin's innocence away.
Well may they rise, while I, whose rustick tongue
80 Ne'er knew to puzzle right, or varnish wrong,
Spurn'd as a beggar, dreaded as a spy,
Live unregarded, unlamented die.
    For what but social guilt the friend endears?
Who shares Orgilio's crimes, his fortune shares.

---

59 *warbling eunuchs:* The Italian opera was then very popular.   *licens'd stage:* By an act of 1737 all plays had to be licensed before performance.

70 i.e. to expose the plagiarism of a titled poet.

72 *Gazetteer:* "The paper which at that time contained apologies for the Court" (Johnson). *The Daily Gazetteer*, the official newspaper of Walpole's ministry, was founded in 1735.

74 *H——y's:* i.e. Hervey's. Lord Hervey, a supporter of Walpole, was the original of Pope's "Sporus" in the *Epistle to Dr. Arbuthnot*.

77 *address:* "skill, dexterity" (*Dictionary*).

84 *Orgilio:* The name implies a person of swollen pride.

85 But thou, should tempting villainy present
    All Marlb'rough hoarded, or all Villiers spent,
    Turn from the glitt'ring bribe thy scornful eye,
    Nor sell for gold, what gold could never buy,
    The peaceful slumber, self-approving day,
90 Unsullied fame, and conscience ever gay.
        The cheated nation's happy fav'rites, see!
    Mark whom the great caress, who frown on me!
    LONDON! the needy villain's gen'ral home,
    The common shore of Paris and of Rome;
95 With eager thirst, by folly or by fate,
    Sucks in the dregs of each corrupted state.
    Forgive my transports on a theme like this,
    I cannot bear a French metropolis.
        Illustrious EDWARD! from the realms of day,
100 The land of heroes and of saints survey;
    Nor hope the British lineaments to trace,
    The rustick grandeur, or the surly grace,
    But lost in thoughtless ease, and empty show,
    Behold the warrior dwindled to a beau;
105 Sense, freedom, piety, refin'd away,
    Of France the mimick, and of Spain the prey.
        All that at home no more can beg or steal,

86 *Marlb'rough . . . Villiers:* Johnson, in his *Life of Swift*, said that the War of the Spanish Succession was "unnecessarily protracted to fill the pockets of Marlborough". In *The Examiner* (No. 16, Thursday, November 23, 1710), Swift reckoned that whereas a successful Roman general was rewarded to the extent of £994 11s. 10d. from the public purse, Marlborough got £540,000! John Churchill (1650-1722) was the first Duke of Marlborough. George Villiers (1628-87), was the second Duke of Buckingham. He was the "Zimri" of Dryden's *Absalom and Achitophel*, and Pope described his miserable end in his Epistle *Of the Use of Riches*, ll. 299-314.

94 *common shore:* common sewer. Cf. Shakespeare's *Pericles*, IV. vi: 190 f. "Empty/Old receptacles, or common shores, of filth."

98 This corresponds to Juvenal's complaints against the Greeks, in the *Third Satire*, ll. 60 sq.

99 EDWARD: Edward III, victor at Crécy.

Or like a gibbet better than a wheel;
Hiss'd from the stage, or hooted from the court,
110 Their air, their dress, their politicks import;
Obsequious, artful, voluble and gay,
On Britain's fond credulity they prey.
No gainful trade their industry can 'scape,
They sing, they dance, clean shoes, or cure a clap;
115 All sciences a fasting Monsieur knows,
And bid him go to hell, to hell he goes.
    Ah! what avails it, that, from slav'ry far,
I drew the breath of life in English air;
Was early taught a Briton's right to prize,
120 And lisp the tale of HENRY's victories;
If the gull'd conqueror receives the chain,
And flattery subdues when arms are vain?
    Studious to please, and ready to submit,
The supple Gaul was born a parasite:
125 Still to his int'rest true, where'er he goes,
Wit, brav'ry, worth, his lavish tongue bestows;
In ev'ry face a thousand graces shine,
From ev'ry tongue flows harmony divine.
These arts in vain our rugged natives try,
130 Strain out with fault'ring diffidence a lye,
And get a kick for awkward flattery.
    Besides, with justice, this discerning age
Admires their wond'rous talents for the stage:
Well may they venture on the mimick's art,
135 Who play from morn to night a borrow'd part;
Practis'd their master's notions to embrace,
Repeat his maxims, and reflect his face;
With ev'ry wild absurdity comply,

---

108 *wheel:* Breaking on the wheel was the method of capital punishment in France until the Revolution.

114 *clap:* venereal disease.

120 HENRY: Henry V, victor at Agincourt.

124 ff. With this passage on the French compare Goldsmith's remarks in *The Traveller*, 239-80.

And view each object with another's eye;
140 To shake with laughter ere the jest they hear,
To pour at will the counterfeited tear,
And as their patron hints the cold or heat,
To shake in dog-days, in December sweat.
   How, when competitors like these contend,
145 Can surly virtue hope to fix a friend?
Slaves that with serious impudence beguile,
And lye without a blush, without a smile;
Exalt each trifle, ev'ry vice adore,
Your taste in snuff, your judgment in a whore;
150 Can Balbo's eloquence applaud, and swear
He gropes his breeches with a monarch's air.
   For arts like these preferr'd, admir'd, caress'd,
They first invade your table, then your breast;
Explore your secrets with insidious art,
155 Watch the weak hour, and ransack all the heart;
Then soon your ill-plac'd confidence repay,
Commence your lords, and govern or betray.
   By numbers here from shame or censure free,
All crimes are safe, but hated poverty.
160 This, only this, the rigid law pursues,
This, only this, provokes the snarling muse.
The sober trader at a tatter'd cloak,
Wakes from his dream, and labours for a joke;
With brisker air the silken courtiers gaze,
165 And turn the varied taunt a thousand ways.
Of all the griefs that harrass the distress'd,
Sure the most bitter is a scornful jest;
Fate never wounds more deep the gen'rous heart,
Than when a blockhead's insult points the dart.
170   Has heaven reserv'd, in pity to the poor,

143 *dog-days:* The dog-days, from July 3 to August 11 in current almanacs, are considered to be the hottest and most unwholesome period of the year for Europeans. See the note on line 16 of the *Translation of Horace* above.
150 *Balbo:* The name implies a stammerer.
157 *Commence your lords:* i.e. begin to be your lords.

No pathless waste, or undiscover'd shore;
No secret island in the boundless main?
No peaceful desart yet unclaim'd by SPAIN?
Quick let us rise, the happy seats explore,
175 And bear oppression's insolence no more.
This mournful truth is ev'ry where confess'd,
SLOW RISES WORTH, BY POVERTY DEPRESS'D:
But here more slow, where all are slaves to gold,
Where looks are merchandise, and smiles are sold;
180 Where won by bribes, by flatteries implor'd,
The groom retails the favours of his lord.
　　But hark! th' affrighted crowd's tumultuous cries
Roll thro' the streets, and thunder to the skies;
Rais'd from some pleasing dream of wealth and pow'r,
185 Some pompous palace, or some blissful bow'r,
Aghast you start, and scarce with aking sight
Sustain th' approaching fire's tremendous light;
Swift from pursuing horrors take your way,
And leave your little ALL to flames a prey;
190 Then thro' the world a wretched vagrant roam,
For where can starving merit find a home?
In vain your mournful narrative disclose,
While all neglect, and most insult your woes.
　　Should heaven's just bolts Orgilio's wealth confound,
195 And spread his flaming palace on the ground,
Swift o'er the land the dismal rumour flies,
And publick mournings pacify the skies;
The laureat tribe in servile verse relate,
How virtue wars with persecuting fate;
200 With well-feign'd gratitude the pension'd band
Refund the plunder of the beggar'd land.
See! while he builds, the gaudy vassals come,

173 "The Spaniards at this time were said to make claim to some of our American provinces" (Johnson). See the notes to lines 30 and 54.
174 *seat:* "situation; site" (*Dictionary*).
194 sq. "This was by Hitch a Bookseller justly remarked to be no picture of modern manners, though it might be true at Rome" (Johnson).

And crowd with sudden wealth the rising dome;
The price of boroughs and of souls restore,
205 And raise his treasures higher than before.
Now bless'd with all the baubles of the great,
The polish'd marble, and the shining plate,
Orgilio sees the golden pile aspire,
And hopes from angry heav'n another fire.
210   Could'st thou resign the park and play content,
For the fair banks of Severn or of Trent;
There might'st thou find some elegant retreat,
Some hireling senator's deserted seat;
And stretch thy prospects o'er the smiling land,
215 For less than rent the dungeons of the Strand;
There prune thy walks, support thy drooping flow'rs,
Direct thy rivulets, and twine thy bow'rs;
And, while thy grounds a cheap repast afford,
Despise the dainties of a venal lord:
220 There ev'ry bush with nature's musick rings,
There ev'ry breeze bears health upon its wings;
On all thy hours security shall smile,
And bless thine evening walk and morning toil.
   Prepare for death, if here at night you roam,
225 And sign your will before you sup from home.
Some fiery fop, with new commission vain,

203 *dome:* building. See Johnson's first definition of the word in the *Dictionary*.

210 *content:* contentedly.

212 *elegant:* "pleasing with minor beauties" (*Dictionary*).

215 *dungeons:* cellars. M. Dorothy George (*London Life in the Eighteenth Century*, London, 1925, p. 85) writes: "A house would be occupied by people of different degrees of prosperity and even of different social grades. The very poor, that is, casual labourers, street sellers and the like ... charwomen and those who kept a mangle, as a rule lived in cellars or else in garrets."

219 *venal:* unprincipled, subject to mercenary considerations.

222 *security:* "freedom from care, anxiety, or apprehension" (*Oxford English Dictionary*).

> Who sleeps on brambles till he kills his man;
> Some frolick drunkard, reeling from a feast,
> Provokes a broil, and stabs you for a jest.
230 Yet ev'n these heroes, mischievously gay,
> Lords of the street, and terrors of the way;
> Flush'd as they are with folly, youth and wine,
> Their prudent insults to the poor confine;
> Afar they mark the flambeau's bright approach,
235 And shun the shining train, and golden coach.
>   In vain, these dangers past, your doors you close,
> And hope the balmy blessings of repose:
> Cruel with guilt, and daring with despair,
> The midnight murd'rer bursts the faithless bar;
240 Invades the sacred hour of silent rest,
> And leaves, unseen, a dagger in your breast.
>   Scarce can our fields, such crowds at Tyburn die,
> With hemp the gallows and the fleet supply.
> Propose your schemes, ye Senatorian band,
245 Whose Ways and Means support the sinking land;
> Lest ropes be wanting in the tempting spring,
> To rig another convoy for the k——g.
>   A single jail, in ALFRED's golden reign,
> Could half the nation's criminals contain;
250 Fair Justice then, without constraint ador'd,
> Held high the steady scale, but deep'd the sword;

229 *broil:* "A tumult; a quarrel" (*Dictionary*).

234 *flambeau:* a torch, usually made of thick wick dipped in wax.

242 *Tyburn* remained the place in London where criminals were hanged till 1783.

245 *Ways and Means:* "A cant term in the House of Commons for methods of raising money" (Johnson).

246-7 These lines refer to the nation's displeasure at the king's visits to Hanover.

251 Compare the traditional picture of Justice, holding the sword with the point resting on the ground. It is possible that Johnson wrote "drop'd" in the sense of "lowered".

No spies were paid, no special juries known,
Blest age! but ah! how diff'rent from our own!
Much could I add,—but see the boat at hand,
255 The tide retiring, calls me from the land:
Farewell!—When youth, and health, and fortune spent,
Thou fly'st for refuge to the wilds of Kent;
And tir'd like me with follies and with crimes,
In angry numbers warn'st succeeding times;
260 Then shall thy friend, nor thou refuse his aid,
Still foe to vice, forsake his Cambrian shade;
In virtue's cause once more exert his rage,
Thy satire point, and animate thy page.

252 *special jury:* "a jury consisting of persons who . . . are of a certain station in society, as esquires, bankers or merchants, or occupy a house . . . of a certain rateable value" (*Oxford English Dictionary*).

An Epitaph on Claudy Phillips, a Musician

CHARLES CLAUDIUS PHILLIPS, a violinist, died in 1732. An epitaph by a Dr. Wilkes was repeated to Johnson by Garrick. Johnson "said to Garrick, 'I think, Davy, I can make a better.' Then, stirring about his tea for a little while, in a state of meditation, he almost extempore produced the following verses" (*Life*, I, 148). Johnson's lines were first printed in *The Gentleman's Magazine*, September 1740.

Phillips! whose touch harmonious could remove
The pangs of guilty pow'r, and hapless love,
Rest here distrest by poverty no more,
Find here that calm thou gav'st so oft before;
Sleep undisturb'd within this peaceful shrine,
Till angels wake thee with a note like thine.

An Ode on Friendship

PROBABLY written before 1740, and possibly several years earlier, the *Ode on Friendship* was first published in *The Gentleman's Magazine*, July 1743. The poem seems to have been popular, as many manuscript copies existed; only one, however, has survived, a copy made by Lady Mary Wortley Montagu.

Friendship! peculiar boon of heav'n,
  The noble mind's delight and pride,
To Men and Angels only giv'n,
  To all the lower world deny'd;

5 While Love, a stranger to the blest,
  Parent of thousand wild desires,
The human and the savage breast
  Inflames alike with raging fires.

With bright, but oft destructive gleam,
10   Alike o'er all his lightnings fly;
Thy lambent glories only beam
  Around the fav'rites of the sky.

Directress of the brave and just,
  O guide me through life's darksome way,
15 And let the tortures of mistrust
  On selfish bosoms only prey.

Thy gentle flows of guiltless joys
  On fools and villains ne'er descend;
In vain for thee the monarch sighs,
20   And hugs a flatterer for a friend.

When Virtues kindred Virtues meet,
  And sister souls together join,
Thy pleasures, permanent as great,
  Are all transporting, all divine.

25 Oh, must their ardours cease to glow
      When souls to blissful climes remove?
    What rais'd our Virtues here below,
      Shall aid our Happiness above.

To Miss ———

On her giving the Author a Gold and Silk net-work Purse of her own weaving

JOHNSON probably wrote this poem on behalf of a friend, Henry Hervey. It was first published in *The Gentleman's Magazine*, May 1747, without Johnson's signature.

    Though gold and silk their charms unite,
    To make thy curious web delight,
    In vain the vary'd work would shine,
    If wrought by any hand but thine,
5 Thy hand that knows the subtler art,
    To weave those nets that catch the heart.
      Spread out by me, the roving coin,
    Thy nets may catch, but not confine,
    Nor can I hope thy silken chain
10 The glitt'ring vagrants shall restrain;
    Why, SYLVIA, was it then decreed,
    The heart, once caught, should ne'er be freed?

Epitaph on Sir Thomas Hanmer

SIR THOMAS HANMER, who had been Speaker of the House of Commons (the "senate" of line 19), died in 1746. Johnson's lines are based on a Latin epitaph written by Robert Freind, who had been Hanmer's tutor at Oxford. The poem first appeared in *The Gentleman's Magazine*, May 1747.

Thou, who survey'st these walls with curious eye,
Pause at this tomb where HANMER's ashes lie;
His various worth, through varied life attend,
And learn his virtues, while thou mourn'st his end.
  His force of genius burn'd in early youth,
With thirst of knowledge, and with love of truth;
His learning, join'd with each endearing art,
Charm'd ev'ry ear, and gain'd on ev'ry heart.
  Thus early wise, th' endanger'd realm to aid,
His country call'd him from the studious shade;
In life's first bloom his publick toils began,
At once commenc'd the Senator and Man.
  In bus'ness dext'rous, weighty in debate,
Thrice ten long years he labour'd for the State;
In ev'ry speech persuasive wisdom flow'd,
In ev'ry act refulgent virtue glow'd.
Suspended faction ceas'd from rage and strife,
To hear his eloquence, and praise his life.
  Resistless merit fix'd the Senate's choice,
Who hail'd him Speaker, with united voice.
Illustrious age! how bright thy glories shone,
When HANMER fill'd the chair, and ANN the throne.
  Then, when dark arts obscur'd each fierce debate,
When mutual frauds perplex'd the maze of State,
The moderator firmly mild appear'd,
Beheld with love, with veneration heard.
  This task perform'd, he sought no gainful post,
Nor wish'd to glitter at his country's cost;
Strict, on the right he fix'd his steadfast eye,
With temp'rate zeal, and wise anxiety;
Nor e'er from virtue's path was lur'd aside,
To pluck the flow'rs of pleasure or of pride.
  Her gifts despis'd, corruption blush'd and fled,
And fame pursu'd him, where conviction led.
  Age call'd at length his active mind to rest,
With honour sated, and with cares opprest;

34 *conviction:* "state of being convinced" (*Dictionary*).

To letter'd ease retir'd, and honest mirth,
To rural grandeur, and domestick worth;
Delighted still to please mankind, or mend,
40 The Patriot's fire yet sparkled in the friend.
   Calm conscience then his former life survey'd,
And recollected toils endear'd the shade;
Till nature call'd him to the gen'ral doom,
And virtue's sorrow dignify'd his tomb.

37 Hanmer's edition of *The Works of Shakespeare in Six Volumes* appeared in 1743-4.

Prologue

Spoken by MR. GARRICK
At the opening of the Theatre in Drury Lane 1747

"THIS year his old pupil and friend, David Garrick, having become joint patentee and manager of Drury Lane Theatre, Johnson honoured his opening of it with a Prologue...." (*Life*). This piece is of interest as indicating Johnson's views on English drama between Shakespeare's time and his own. It was printed separately in 1747.

When Learning's Triumph o'er her barb'rous Foes
First rear'd the Stage, immortal SHAKESPEAR rose;
Each Change of many-colour'd Life he drew,
Exhausted Worlds, and then imagin'd new:
5 Existence saw him spurn her bounded Reign,
And panting Time toil'd after him in vain:
His pow'rful Strokes presiding Truth impress'd,
And unresisted Passion storm'd the Breast.
   Then JOHNSON came, instructed from the School,
10 To please in Method, and invent by Rule;
His studious Patience, and laborious Art,
By regular Approach essay'd the Heart;

9 JOHNSON: Ben Jonson (1572-1637), author of *The Alchemist*, etc.

>   Cold Approbation gave the ling'ring Bays,
>   For those who durst not censure, scarce cou'd praise.
> 15   A Mortal born he met the general Doom,
>   But left, like *Egypt*'s Kings, a lasting Tomb.
>   The Wits of *Charles* found easier Ways to Fame,
>   Nor wish'd for JOHNSON's Art, or SHAKESPEAR's Flame;
>   Themselves they studied, as they felt, they writ,
> 20   Intrigue was Plot, Obscenity was Wit.
>   Vice always found a sympathetick Friend;
>   They pleas'd their Age, and did not aim to mend.
>   Yet Bards like these aspir'd to lasting Praise,
>   And proudly hop'd to pimp in future Days.
> 25   Their Cause was gen'ral, their Supports were strong,
>   Their Slaves were willing, and their Reign was long;
>   Till Shame regain'd the Post that Sense betray'd,
>   And Virtue call'd Oblivion to her Aid.
>   Then crush'd by Rules, and weaken'd as refin'd,
> 30   For Years the Pow'r of Tragedy declin'd;
>   From Bard, to Bard, the frigid Caution crept,
>   Till Declamation roar'd, while Passion slept.
>   Yet still did Virtue deign the Stage to tread,
>   Philosophy remain'd, though Nature fled.
> 35   But forc'd at length her antient Reign to quit,
>   She saw great *Faustus* lay the Ghost of Wit:
>   Exulting Folly hail'd the joyful Day,

13 *Bays:* fame, reputation. The leaves or sprigs of the bay-laurel were, in classical times, woven into a garland to reward poets.

17 This reminds one of Pope's comment on "the wits of either Charles's days,/The mob of gentlemen who wrote with ease". *Epistle to Augustus*, ll. 107-8.

24 *to pimp:* to minister to anything evil, especially base appetites.

36 It was customary to act a farce after the performance of a tragedy. Even *The Life and Death of Dr. Faustus* (the subject of Marlowe's great play) was turned into a farce. In 1723 Thurmond's *Harlequin Doctor Faustus* was performed at Drury Lane, and *The Necromancer: or, Harlequin's Doctor Faustus* at Lincoln's Inn Fields. (See Pope, *The Dunciad*, ed. J. Sutherland, vol. V of the Twickenham edition, 3rd edition revised, 1963, p. 176.)

And Pantomime, and Song, confirm'd her Sway.
But who the coming Changes can presage,
40 And mark the future Periods of the Stage?—
Perhaps if Skill could distant Times explore,
New *Behns*, new *Durfeys*, yet remain in Store.
Perhaps, where *Lear* has rav'd, and *Hamlet* dy'd,
On flying Cars new Sorcerers may ride.
45 Perhaps, for who can guess th' Effects of Chance?
Here *Hunt* may box, or *Mahomet* may dance.
Hard is his lot, that here by Fortune plac'd,
Must watch the wild Vicissitudes of Taste;
With ev'ry Meteor of Caprice must play,
50 And chase the new-blown Bubbles of the Day.
Ah! let not Censure term our Fate our Choice,
The Stage but echoes back the publick Voice.
The Drama's Laws the Drama's Patrons give,
For we that live to please, must please to live.
55 Then prompt no more the Follies you decry,
As Tyrants doom their Tools of Guilt to die;
'Tis yours this Night to bid the Reign commence
Of rescu'd Nature, and reviving Sense;
To chase the Charms of Sound, the Pomp of Show,
60 For useful Mirth, and salutary Woe,
Bid scenic Virtue form the rising Age,
And Truth diffuse her Radiance from the Stage.

42 *Behns:* Aphra Behn (1640-89) was a popular dramatist and novelist—"gay, witty and coarse". *Durfeys:* Tom D'Urfey (1653-1723) was a dramatist and humorous poet, and, according to Alexandre Beljame, "the professional jester and recognised buffoon of all the young scatter-brains of Charles's Court".

46 *Hunt:* Edward Hunt, a light-weight pugilist. *Mahomet* was a rope-dancer, who had performed at Covent Garden Theatre.

The Vanity of Human Wishes

The Tenth SATIRE of JUVENAL Imitated

The Vanity of Human Wishes was published in January 1749, the month before Johnson's tragedy *Irene* was acted at the Theatre Royal in Drury Lane. Garrick said of it: "When Johnson lived much with the Herveys, and saw a good deal of what was passing in life, he wrote his *London*, which is lively and easy. When he became more retired, he gave us his *Vanity of Human Wishes*, which is as hard as Greek. Had he gone on to imitate another satire, it would have been as hard as Hebrew" (*Life*, 1, 194).

Let observation with extensive view,
Survey mankind, from China to Peru;
Remark each anxious toil, each eager strife,
And watch the busy scenes of crouded life;
5 Then say how hope and fear, desire and hate,
O'erspread with snares the clouded maze of fate,
Where wav'ring man, betray'd by vent'rous pride,
To tread the dreary paths without a guide,
As treach'rous phantoms in the mist delude,
10 Shuns fancied ills, or chases airy good;
How rarely reason guides the stubborn choice,
Rules the bold hand, or prompts the suppliant voice;
How nations sink, by darling schemes oppress'd,
When vengeance listens to the fool's request.
15 Fate wings with ev'ry wish th' afflictive dart,
Each gift of nature, and each grace of art,
With fatal heat impetuous courage glows,
With fatal sweetness elocution flows,
Impeachment stops the speaker's pow'rful breath,
20 And restless fire precipitates on death.

15-16 i.e. men's best qualities and abilities are used by fate to bring about their downfall.

20 *And restless . . . death:* The sense is that the restless fire (of genius) hurls the speaker to his doom.

But scarce observ'd, the knowing and the bold
Fall in the gen'ral massacre of gold;
Wide-wasting pest! that rages unconfin'd,
And crouds with crimes the records of mankind;
25 For gold his sword the hireling ruffian draws,
For gold the hireling judge distorts the laws;
Wealth heap'd on wealth, nor truth nor safety buys,
The dangers gather as the treasures rise.
    Let hist'ry tell where rival kings command,
30 And dubious title shakes the madded land,
When statutes glean the refuse of the sword,
How much more safe the vassal than the lord;
Low skulks the hind beneath the rage of pow'r,
And leaves the wealthy traytor in the Tow'r,
35 Untouch'd his cottage, and his slumbers sound,
Tho' confiscation's vulturs hover round.
    The needy traveller, serene and gay,
Walks the wild heath, and sings his toil away.
Does envy seize thee? crush th' upbraiding joy,
40 Increase his riches and his peace destroy;
Now fears in dire vicissitude invade,
The rustling brake alarms, and quiv'ring shade,
Nor light nor darkness bring his pain relief,
One shews the plunder, and one hides the thief.
45   Yet still one gen'ral cry the skies assails,
And gain and grandeur load the tainted gales;
Few know the toiling statesman's fear or care,
Th' insidious rival and the gaping heir.

22 *massacre of gold:* i.e. money is at the root of much evil and violence.

33 *hind:* "A peasant; a boor; a mean rustick" (*Dictionary*).

42 *brake:* "thicket of brambles, or of thorns" (*Dictionary*).

46 *gales:* with this usage, compare Addison in *Spectator*, No. 56: "He felt a Gale of Perfumes breathing upon him."

48 *gaping:* "desiring eagerly, longing to obtain" (*Oxford English Dictionary*). The *gaping heir* is thus one who wishes to supplant the statesman in political power.

Once more, Democritus, arise on earth,
50 With chearful wisdom and instructive mirth,
See motley life in modern trappings dress'd,
And feed with varied fools th' eternal jest:
Thou who couldst laugh where want enchain'd caprice,
Toil crush'd conceit, and man was of a piece;
55 Where wealth unlov'd without a mourner dy'd,
And scarce a sycophant was fed by pride;
Where ne'er was known the form of mock debate,
Or seen a new-made mayor's unwieldy state;
Where change of fav'rites made no change of laws,
60 And senates heard before they judg'd a cause;
How wouldst thou shake at Britain's modish tribe,
Dart the quick taunt, and edge the piercing gibe?
Attentive truth and nature to descry,
And pierce each scene with philosophic eye.
65 To thee were solemn toys or empty shew,
The robes of pleasure and the veils of woe:
All aid the farce, and all thy mirth maintain,
Whose joys are causeless, or whose griefs are vain.
 Such was the scorn that fill'd the sage's mind,
70 Renew'd at ev'ry glance on humankind;
How just that scorn ere yet thy voice declare,
Search every state, and canvass ev'ry pray'r.
 Unnumber'd suppliants croud Preferment's gate,
Athirst for wealth, and burning to be great;
75 Delusive Fortune hears th' incessant call,
They mount, they shine, evaporate, and fall.
On ev'ry stage the foes of peace attend,

49 *Democritus:* Democritus of Abdera (460-367 B.C.) was said to have found material for laughter in all human affairs.

51 *motley:* diversified, and always foolish.

54 *conceit:* imagination.

56 *sycophant:* a flattering parasite.

72 *state:* condition of life.

76 The image is of fireworks, and refers back to "burning to be great".

Hate dogs their flight, and insult mocks their end.
Love ends with hope, the sinking statesman's door
80 Pours in the morning worshiper no more;
For growing names the weekly scribbler lies,
To growing wealth the dedicator flies,
From every room descends the painted face,
That hung the bright Palladium of the place,
85 And smoak'd in kitchens, or in auctions sold,
To better features yields the frame of gold;
For now no more we trace in ev'ry line
Heroic worth, benevolence divine:
The form distorted justifies the fall,
90 And detestation rids th' indignant wall.
   But will not Britain hear the last appeal,
Sign her foes doom, or guard her fav'rites zeal?
Through Freedom's sons no more remonstrance rings,
Degrading nobles and controuling kings;
95 Our supple tribes repress their patriot throats,
And ask no questions but the price of votes;
With weekly libels and septennial ale,
Their wish is full to riot and to rail.
   In full-blown dignity, see Wolsey stand,

81 *the weekly scribbler:* i.e. a writer in the political journals, generally published once a week.

82 *dedicator:* "one who inscribes his work to a patron with compliment and servility" (*Dictionary*).

83 *the painted face:* i.e. the portrait.

84 i.e. that hung (there as) the bright Palladium of the place. *Palladium*, which is now used figuratively for anything on which the safety of a city or institution is thought to depend, is from the image of the goddess Pallas in the citadel of Troy. Troy could not be defeated until the image was removed.

Juvenal describes how when Sejanus, favourite of the Emperor Tiberius, fell from power, his statue was melted down into household utensils.

97 *septennial ale:* The length of a Parliament was seven years. Johnson sneers at undignified electioneering tactics, which included bribery with free beer.

100 Law in his voice, and fortune in his hand:
    To him the church, the realm, their pow'rs consign,
    Thro' him the rays of regal bounty shine,
    Turn'd by his nod the stream of honour flows,
    His smile alone security bestows:
105 Still to new heights his restless wishes tow'r,
    Claim leads to claim, and pow'r advances pow'r;
    Till conquest unresisted ceas'd to please,
    And rights submitted, left him none to seize.
    At length his sov'reign frowns—the train of state
110 Mark the keen glance, and watch the sign to hate.
    Where-e'er he turns he meets a stranger's eye,
    His suppliants scorn him, and his followers fly;
    At once is lost the pride of aweful state,
    The golden canopy, the glitt'ring plate,
115 The regal palace, the luxurious board,
    The liv'ried army, and the menial lord.
    With age, with cares, with maladies oppress'd,
    He seeks the refuge of monastic rest.
    Grief aids disease, remember'd folly stings,
120 And his last sighs reproach the faith of kings.
        Speak thou, whose thoughts at humble peace repine,
    Shall Wolsey's wealth, with Wolsey's end be thine?
    Or liv'st thou now, with safer pride content,
    The wisest justice on the banks of Trent?
125 For why did Wolsey near the steeps of fate,

100 *Law in his voice:* Thomas Wolsey (*c.* 1475-1530) was Lord Chancellor. He almost certainly wielded more power than any English subject before or since, and his downfall from such a height made him an impressive illustration of Johnson's theme.

120 Johnson probably has in mind the lines from Shakespeare's *Henry VIII*, at the end of III, ii:

> Had I but serv'd my God with half the zeal
> I serv'd my King, he would not in mine age
> Have left me naked to mine enemies.

The phrase "the faith of kings" may be an ironic reference to Henry's title of "defender of the faith".

THE VANITY OF HUMAN WISHES 45

On weak foundations raise th' enormous weight?
Why but to sink beneath misfortune's blow,
With louder ruin to the gulphs below?
What gave great Villiers to th' assassin's knife,
130 And fixed disease on Harley's closing life?
What murder'd Wentworth, and what exil'd Hyde,
By kings protected, and to kings ally'd?
What but their wish indulg'd in courts to shine,
And pow'r too great to keep, or to resign?
135 When first the college rolls receive his name,
The young enthusiast quits his ease for fame;
Through all his veins the fever of renown
Burns from the strong contagion of the gown;
O'er Bodley's dome his future labours spread,
140 And Bacon's mansion trembles o'er his head.
Are these thy views? proceed, illustrious youth,
And virtue guard thee to the throne of Truth!
Yet should thy soul indulge the gen'rous heat,
Till captive Science yields her last retreat;

129 *Villiers:* George Villiers, the first Duke of Buckingham, father of the "Villiers" of *London*, l. 86. He was stabbed to death in 1628. **130** *Harley:* Robert Harley, Earl of Oxford, was leader of the Tory party under Queen Anne. Johnson is probably inaccurate in attributing the bad health of his last years to his fall from political power. **131** *Wentworth:* Thomas Wentworth, Earl of Strafford, who was a minister of Charles I, was impeached and executed in 1641. *Hyde:* Edward Hyde, Earl of Clarendon, who was Charles II's Chancellor, was banished in 1667.

132 *By kings protected:* Wentworth was condemned by Parliament, and Charles I was unable to save him. *to kings ally'd:* Hyde's daughter Anne married the Duke of York, afterwards James II.

139 i.e. his future writings spread throughout the Bodleian library. *dome:* building (as in *London*, l. 203). The University library at Oxford is known as "the Bodleian library" after Sir Thomas Bodley, who restored and endowed it in 1600.

140 The reputed "mansion" of Friar Bacon was the gatehouse of a bridge near Pembroke College, Oxford. Tradition held that it would fall when a man greater than Bacon should pass under the bridge.

144 *Science:* knowledge.

145	Should Reason guide thee with her brightest ray,
	And pour on misty Doubt resistless day;
	Should no false Kindness lure to loose delight,
	Nor Praise relax, nor Difficulty fright;
	Should tempting Novelty thy cell refrain,
150	And Sloth effuse her opiate fumes in vain;
	Should Beauty blunt on fops her fatal dart,
	Nor claim the triumph of a letter'd heart;
	Should no Disease thy torpid veins invade,
	Nor Melancholy's phantoms haunt thy shade;
155	Yet hope not life from grief or danger free,
	Nor think the doom of man revers'd for thee:
	Deign on the passing world to turn thine eyes,
	And pause awhile from letters, to be wise;
	There mark what ills the scholar's life assail,
160	Toil, envy, want, the patron, and the jail.
	See nations slowly wise, and meanly just,
	To buried merit raise the tardy bust.
	If dreams yet flatter, once again attend,
	Hear Lydiat's life, and Galileo's end.
165	Nor deem, when learning her last prize bestows,
	The glitt'ring eminence exempt from foes;
	See when the vulgar 'scape, despis'd or aw'd,
	Rebellion's vengeful talons seize on Laud.

153 *torpid:* sluggish.

160 *patron:* The first edition had 'Garret'. If the reader will look up Johnson's justly famous letter to Lord Chesterfield, the reason for the change will be obvious.

164 *Lydiat:* Thomas Lydiat (1572-1646). In spite of a European reputation for his works on chronology, he lived and died in poverty.   *Galileo:* Galileo Galilei (1564-1642), Italian astronomer and scientist. He came into conflict with the Papal authority for upholding the truth of the Copernican system, and was forced to abjure his beliefs as a scientist. There is some doubt as to whether he was actually tortured.

168 *Laud:* William Laud (1573-1645), Archbishop of Canterbury, was executed by the Parliamentarians. However, it was not "fatal Learning" which brought about his downfall, but his uncompromising attitude in ecclesiastical matters.

THE VANITY OF HUMAN WISHES 47

      From meaner minds, tho' smaller fines content,
170 The plunder'd palace or sequester'd rent;
      Mark'd out by dangerous parts he meets the shock,
      And fatal Learning leads him to the block:
      Around his tomb let Art and Genius weep,
      But hear his death, ye blockheads, hear and sleep.
175   The festal blazes, the triumphal show,
      The ravish'd standard, and the captive foe,
      The senate's thanks, the gazette's pompous tale,
      With force resistless o'er the brave prevail.
      Such bribes the rapid Greek o'er Asia whirl'd,
180 For such the steady Romans shook the world;
      For such in distant lands the Britons shine,
      And stain with blood the Danube or the Rhine;
      This pow'r has praise, that virtue scarce can warm,
      Till fame supplies the universal charm.
185 Yet Reason frowns on War's unequal game,
      Where wasted nations raise a single name,
      And mortgag'd states their grandsires wreaths regret,
      From age to age in everlasting debt;
      Wreaths which at last the dear-bought right convey
190 To rust on medals, or on stones decay.
        On what foundation stands the warrior's pride,
      How just his hopes let Swedish Charles decide;
      A frame of adamant, a soul of fire,

169 *content:* i.e. content the persecutor.
170 *sequester'd:* sequestrated, diverted from its owner.
171 *parts:* "Qualities; powers; faculties" (*Dictionary*).
177 *gazette's:* commonly accented on the first syllable in the eighteenth century.
180 F. R. Leavis comments: "That 'steady' turns the vague *cliché*, 'shook the world' into the felt percussion of tramping legions." *Revaluation*, p. 118.
183-4 Praise is more powerful than virtue unaccompanied by fame.
187 *wreaths:* triumphal garlands.
192 *Swedish Charles:* Charles XII of Sweden (1682-1718). Johnson had thought of writing a play about him, and his interest in Charles is reflected in this account, one of the finest passages in the poem.

No dangers fright him, and no labours tire;
O'er love, o'er fear, extends his wide domain,
Unconquer'd lord of pleasure and of pain;
No joys to him pacific scepters yield,
War sounds the trump, he rushes to the field;
Behold surrounding kings their pow'r combine,
And one capitulate, and one resign;
Peace courts his hand, but spreads her charms in vain;
"Think nothing gain'd," he cries, "till nought remain,
"On Moscow's walls till Gothic standards fly,
"And all be mine beneath the polar sky."
The march begins in military state,
And nations on his eye suspended wait;
Stern Famine guards the solitary coast,
And Winter barricades the realms of Frost;
He comes, not want and cold his course delay;—
Hide, blushing Glory, hide Pultowa's day:
The vanquish'd hero leaves his broken bands,
And shews his miseries in distant lands;
Condemn'd a needy supplicant to wait,
While ladies interpose, and slaves debate.
But did not Chance at length her error mend?
Did no subverted empire mark his end?
Did rival monarchs give the fatal wound?
Or hostile millions press him to the ground?
His fall was destin'd to a barren strand,
A petty fortress, and a dubious hand;
He left the name, at which the world grew pale,
To point a moral, or adorn a tale.
    All times their scenes of pompous woes afford,

202 *till nought remain:* i.e. to be achieved.
203 *Gothic:* i.e. Swedish (Gothland).
208 The European winter of 1708 was the severest for a century.
210 *Pultowa's day:* Charles was defeated by Peter the Great at Pultowa in 1709.
220 *a dubious hand:* It was suspected that Charles was killed by a stray bullet fired by one of his own men.

THE VANITY OF HUMAN WISHES

From Persia's tyrant to Bavaria's lord.
225 In gay hostility, and barb'rous pride,
With half mankind embattled at his side,
Great Xerxes comes to seize the certain prey,
And starves exhausted regions in his way;
Attendant Flatt'ry counts his myriads o'er,
230 Till counted myriads sooth his pride no more;
Fresh praise is try'd till madness fires his mind,
The waves he lashes, and enchains the wind;
New pow'rs are claim'd, new pow'rs are still bestow'd,
Till rude resistance lops the spreading god;
235 The daring Greeks deride the martial show,
And heap their vallies with the gaudy foe;
Th' insulted sea with humbler thoughts he gains,
A single skiff to speed his flight remains;
Th' incumber'd oar scarce leaves the dreaded coast
240 Through purple billows and a floating host.
    The bold Bavarian, in a luckless hour,
Tries the dread summits of Cesarean pow'r,
With unexpected legions bursts away,
And sees defenceless realms receive his sway;
245 Short sway! fair Austria spreads her mournful charms,
The queen, the beauty, sets the world in arms;
From hill to hill the beacons rousing blaze

224 *Persia's tyrant:* Xerxes I, King of Persia (485-464 B.C.) set out with a large fleet and army to crush Greece. In Thrace the gallant band of three hundred Spartans vainly tried to halt them at the pass of Thermopylae—one of the great incidents of military history. The decisive battle took place in the narrow strait between the island of Salamis and the mainland of Attica. In this confined space, the size of the Persian fleet made it unwieldy, and Xerxes saw it utterly routed.   *Bavaria's lord:* Charles Albert, Elector of Bavaria, asserted his claim to the imperial throne in 1740, and was crowned as Charles VII in 1742. He was merely a puppet emperor and died, worn out by his troubles, in 1745.

245 *fair Austria:* Maria Theresa. Johnson wrote an account of the war of the Austrian succession and the part played in it by Maria Theresa in his "Memoirs of Frederick III, King of Prussia", published in *The Literary Magazine*, 1756.

>   Spreads wide the hope of plunder and of praise;
>   The fierce Croatian, and the wild Hussar,
> 250 And all the sons of ravage croud the war;
>   The baffled prince in honour's flatt'ring bloom
>   Of hasty greatness finds the fatal doom,
>   His foes derision, and his subjects blame,
>   And steals to death from anguish and from shame.
> 255   Enlarge my life with multitude of days,
>   In health, in sickness, thus the suppliant prays;
>   Hides from himself his state, and shuns to know,
>   That life protracted is protracted woe.
>   Time hovers o'er, impatient to destroy,
> 260 And shuts up all the passages of joy:
>   In vain their gifts the bounteous seasons pour,
>   The fruit autumnal, and the vernal flow'r,
>   With listless eyes the dotard views the store,
>   He views, and wonders that they please no more;
> 265 Now pall the tasteless meats, and joyless wines,
>   And Luxury with sighs her slave resigns.
>   Approach, ye minstrels, try the soothing strain,
>   Diffuse the tuneful lenitives of pain:
>   No sounds alas would touch th' impervious ear,
> 270 Though dancing mountains witness'd Orpheus near;
>   Nor lute nor lyre his feeble pow'rs attend,
>   Nor sweeter musick of a virtuous friend,
>   But everlasting dictates croud his tongue,
>   Perversely grave, or positively wrong.
> 275 The still returning tale, and ling'ring jest,
>   Perplex the fawning niece and pamper'd guest,

249 *fierce Croatian:* The Croats were a byword for barbaric behaviour in warfare. In Fielding's *Tom Jones* (VI, ii), Mrs. Western calls her brother, Squire Western, "absolutely a perfect Croat". *Hussar:* The word is here used in its strict sense of "a Hungarian light-horseman".

268 *lenitives:* palliatives.

270 The legendary Orpheus was held to be so marvellous a musician that wild beasts and even trees and rivers came to hear him.

271 *attend:* attend to, regard. The subject is of course *pow'rs*.

While growing hopes scarce awe the gath'ring sneer,
And scarce a legacy can bribe to hear;
The watchful guests still hint the last offence,
280　The daughter's petulance, the son's expence,
Improve his heady rage with treach'rous skill,
And mould his passions till they make his will.
　Unnumber'd maladies his joints invade,
Lay siege to life and press the dire blockade;
285　But unextinguish'd Avarice still remains,
And dreaded losses aggravate his pains;
He turns, with anxious heart and cripled hands,
His bonds of debt, and mortgages of lands;
Or views his coffers with suspicious eyes,
290　Unlocks his gold, and counts it till he dies.
　But grant, the virtues of a temp'rate prime
Bless with an age exempt from scorn or crime;
An age that melts with unperceiv'd decay,
And glides in modest Innocence away;
295　Whose peaceful day Benevolence endears,
Whose night congratulating Conscience cheers;
The gen'ral fav'rite as the gen'ral friend:
Such age there is, and who shall wish its end?
　Yet ev'n on this her load Misfortune flings,
300　To press the weary minutes flagging wings:
New sorrow rises as the day returns,
A sister sickens, or a daughter mourns.
Now kindred Merit fills the sable bier,
Now lacerated Friendship claims a tear.
305　Year chases year, decay pursues decay,
Still drops some joy from with'ring life away;
New forms arise, and diff'rent views engage,
Superfluous lags the vet'ran on the stage,
Till pitying Nature signs the last release,
310　And bids afflicted worth retire to peace.
　But few there are whom hours like these await,

280 *expence:* extravagance.
281 *Improve:* augment.

Who set unclouded in the gulphs of fate.
From Lydia's monarch should the search descend,
By Solon caution'd to regard his end,
315 In life's last scene what prodigies surprise,
Fears of the brave, and follies of the wise?
From Marlb'rough's eyes the streams of dotage flow,
And Swift expires a driv'ler and a show.
 The teeming mother, anxious for her race,
320 Begs for each birth the fortune of a face:
Yet Vane could tell what ills from beauty spring;
And Sedley curs'd the form that pleas'd a king.
Ye nymphs of rosy lips and radiant eyes,
Whom Pleasure keeps too busy to be wise,
325 Whom Joys with soft varieties invite,
By day the frolick, and the dance by night,
Who frown with vanity, who smile with art,
And ask the latest fashion of the heart,
What care, what rules your heedless charms shall save,
330 Each nymph your rival, and each youth your slave?
Against your fame with fondness hate combines,
The rival batters, and the lover mines.
With distant voice neglected Virtue calls,
Less heard and less, the faint remonstrance falls;
335 Tir'd with contempt, she quits the slipp'ry reign,
And Pride and Prudence take her seat in vain.
In croud at once, where none the pass defend,

313 *Lydia's monarch:* Croesus (reigned 560-546 B.C.) was fabulously wealthy. Solon, the Athenian, told him that no man could be accounted happy until he had ended his life happily. See Herodotus, *History*, I, 30-3. *descend:* i.e. from antiquity to modern times.

317 Marlborough, who died in 1722, suffered two paralytic strokes in 1716. From 1742 until his death in 1745 Swift was a helpless wreck. See Johnson's *Life of Swift*.

321 *Vane:* Anne Vane (d. 1736) was mistress to Frederick Prince of Wales.

322 *Sedley:* Catherine Sedley (1657-1717) was mistress to the Duke of York, afterwards James II.

The harmless Freedom, and the private Friend.
The guardians yield, by force superior ply'd;
340 By Int'rest, Prudence; and by Flatt'ry, Pride.
Now beauty falls betray'd, despis'd, distress'd,
And hissing Infamy proclaims the rest.
  Where then shall Hope and Fear their objects find?
Must dull Suspence corrupt the stagnant mind?
345 Must helpless man, in ignorance sedate,
Roll darkling down the torrent of his fate?
Must no dislike alarm, no wishes rise,
No cries attempt the mercies of the skies?
Enquirer, cease, petitions yet remain,
350 Which heav'n may hear, nor deem religion vain.
Still raise for good the supplicating voice,
But leave to heav'n the measure and the choice,
Safe in his pow'r, whose eyes discern afar
The secret ambush of a specious pray'r.
355 Implore his aid, in his decisions rest,
Secure whate'er he gives, he gives the best.
Yet when the sense of sacred presence fires,
And strong devotion to the skies aspires,
Pour forth thy fervours for a healthful mind,
360 Obedient passions, and a will resign'd;
For love, which scarce collective man can fill;
For patience sov'reign o'er transmuted ill;
For faith, that panting for a happier seat,
Counts death kind Nature's signal of retreat:
365 These goods for man the laws of heav'n ordain,
These goods he grants, who grants the pow'r to gain;
With these celestial wisdom calms the mind,
And makes the happiness she does not find.

346 *darkling:* "Being in the dark; being without light: a word merely poetical" (*Dictionary*).

A New Prologue spoken at the Representation of Comus

Comus was presented at Drury Lane on April 5, 1750, for the benefit of Mrs. Elizabeth Foster, Milton's grand-daughter, and only surviving descendant. Johnson, hearing that this woman was living in poverty, persuaded Garrick to give a performance on her behalf. The profits were £130. The prologue was printed separately in 1750.

    Ye patriot Crouds, who burn for *England*'s Fame,
    Ye Nymphs, whose Bosoms beat at MILTON'S Name,
    Whose gen'rous Zeal, unbought by flatt'ring Rhimes,
    Shames the mean Pensions of *Augustan* Times;
5 Immortal Patrons of succeeding Days,
    Attend this Prelude of perpetual Praise!
    Let Wit, condemn'd the feeble War to wage
    With close Malevolence, or public Rage;
    Let Study, worn with Virtue's fruitless Lore,
10 Behold this Theatre, and grieve no more.
    This Night, distinguish'd by your Smile, shall tell,
    That never BRITON can in vain excel;
    The slighted Arts Futurity shall trust,
    And rising Ages hasten to be just.
15   At length our mighty Bard's victorious Lays
    Fill the loud Voice of universal Praise,
    And baffled Spite, with hopeless Anguish dumb,
    Yields to Renown the Centuries to come.
    With ardent Haste, each Candidate of Fame
20 Ambitious catches at his tow'ring Name:
    He sees, and pitying sees, vain Wealth bestow
    Those pageant Honours which he scorn'd below:
    While Crowds aloft the laureat Bust behold,
    Or trace his Form on circulating Gold,

24 *circulating Gold:* medals, bearing Milton's likeness, and struck in his honour.

25 Unknown, unheeded, long his Offspring lay,
    And Want hung threat'ning o'er her slow Decay.
    What tho' she shine with no MILTONIAN Fire,
    No fav'ring Muse her morning Dreams inspire;
    Yet softer Claims the melting Heart engage,
30 Her Youth laborious, and her blameless Age:
    Hers the mild Merits of domestic Life,
    The patient Suff'rer, and the faithful Wife.
    Thus grac'd with humble Virtue's native Charms
    Her Grandsire leaves her in *Britannia*'s Arms,
35 Secure with Peace, with Competence, to dwell,
    While tutelary Nations guard her Cell.
    Yours is the Charge, ye Fair, ye Wise, ye Brave!
    'Tis yours to crown Desert—beyond the Grave!

Translations from Boethius

DE CONSOLATIONE PHILOSOPHIAE

AURICIUS MANLIUS SEVERINUS BOETHIUS (c. A.D. 480-524), was the author of the *De Consolatione*, a discussion in dialogue form of the problems of moral responsibility, which was extremely influential, and was translated by King Alfred, Chaucer, Queen Elizabeth and many others. Johnson, typically, abandoned work on his translation when he learned that a needy author was engaged on the same project. Of the passages reproduced here, only the first was printed in the eighteenth century—in *The Edinburgh Magazine*, April 1788.

BOOK II. METRE 2

Though countless as the Grains of Sand
That roll at Eurus loud command;
Though countless as the lamps of night
That glad us with vicarious light;

2 *Eurus:* the South-East Wind.

4 *vicarious:* taking the place of (the Sun). The *Oxford English Dictionary* gives a quotation dated 1709: "God made the moon a vicarious Light to the Sun."

5   Fair plenty, gracious Queen, shou'd pour
    The blessings of a golden Show'r,
    Not all the gifts of Fate combin'd
    Would ease the hunger of the mind,
    But swallowing all the mighty Store,
10 Rapacity would call for more;
    For still where wishes most abound
    Unquench'd the thirst of gain is found;
    In vain the shining Gifts are sent,
    For none are rich without content.

Book II. Metre 4

Wouldst thou to some stedfast Seat,
Out of Fortune's Pow'r retreat?
Wouldst thou when fierce Eurus blows
Calmly rest in safe Repose?
5   Wouldst thou see the foaming Main,
Tossing rave but rave in vain?
Shun the Mountain's airy Brow,
Shun the Sea-sapp'd Sand below;
Soon th' aspiring Fabric falls,
10 When loud Auster shakes her Walls,
Soon the treachrous Sands retreat,
From beneath the cumbrous Weight;
Fix not where the tempting Height
Mingles Danger with Delight;
15 Safe upon the rocky Ground,
Firm and low thy Mansion found;
There, mid Tempests loudest roars,
Dashing Waves and shatter'd Shoars,
Thou shalt sit and smile to see
20 All the World afraid but thee,
Lead a long and peaceful Age,
And deride their utmost Rage.

10 *Auster:* the South-West Wind.

Book III. Metre 5

The Man who pants for ample Sway
Must bid his Passions all obey;
Must bid each wild Desire be still,
Nor yoke his Reason with his Will:
5   For tho' beneath thy haughty Brow
Warm India's supple Sons should bow,
Tho' Northern Climes confess thy Sway,
Which erst in Frost and Freedom lay,
If Sorrow pine or Av'rice crave,
10 Bow down and own thyself a Slave.

Prologue to 'The Good Natur'd Man'

JOHNSON suffered "great perturbation and distraction" in 1768, and was in no mood for writing prologues to comedies. In writing this piece he was keeping a long-standing promise to Goldsmith. (See *Life*, II, 42, 45.) The extended comparison of the dramatist's appeal to his audience with the politician's to his electors is explained by the approaching General Election. The prologue was printed in *The Public Advertiser*, February 3, 1768.

Prest by the load of life, the weary mind
Surveys the general toil of human kind;
With cool submission joins the labouring train,
And social sorrow loses half its pain:
5   Our anxious Bard, without complaint, may share
This bustling season's epidemic care;
Like Caesar's pilot, dignified by fate,
Tost in one common storm with all the great;

7 *Caesar's pilot:* Plutarch tells of Caesar, disguised as a slave, setting out in a small boat for Brundisium to link up with his army. When a storm caused the boat's master to turn back, Caesar revealed his identity: "Go on, my friend . . . you carry Caesar and his fortune in your boat" (Plutarch, *Lives*, Everyman edition, vol. II, pp. 558-9).

Distrest alike, the statesman and the wit,
10 When one a borough courts, and one the pit.
The busy candidates for power and fame,
Have hopes, and fears, and wishes, just the same;
Disabled both to combat, or to fly,
Must hear all taunts, and hear without reply.
15 Uncheck'd on both, loud rabbles vent their rage,
As mongrels bay the lion in a cage.
Th' offended burgess hoards his angry tale,
For that blest year when all that vote may rail;
Their schemes of spite the poet's foes dismiss,
20 Till that glad night when all that hate may hiss.
This day the powder'd curls and golden coat,
Says swelling Crispin, begg'd a cobbler's vote.
This night our wit, the pert apprentice cries,
Lies at my feet, I hiss him, and he dies.
25 The great, 'tis true, can charm th' electing tribe;
The bard may supplicate, but cannot bribe.
Yet judg'd by those, whose voices ne'er were sold,
He feels no want of ill-persuading gold;
But confident of praise, if praise be due,
30 Trusts without fear, to merit, and to you.

22 *swelling Crispin:* a cobbler puffed up with pride. Crispin is the patron-saint of shoemakers.

Epitaph on Hogarth

WILLIAM HOGARTH (1697-1764), was a famous painter and engraver, "a pictorial chronicler of life and manners . . . a satirist and humourist on canvas" (*Dictionary of National Biography*). Mrs. Hogarth asked Garrick for an epitaph upon her husband, and Johnson produced these lines as a model for Garrick to follow. They were sent to Garrick in a letter of December 12, 1771. The first stanza was printed in *The Gentleman's Magazine*, March 1786.

EPITAPH ON HOGARTH

The Hand of Art here torpid lies
   That traced th' essential form of Grace,
Here death has clos'd the curious eyes
   That saw the manners in the Face.

5 If Genius warm thee, Reader, stay,
   If Merit touch thee, shed a tear,
Be Vice and Dulness far away
   Great Hogarth's honour'd Dust is here.

A Short Song of Congratulation

SIR JOHN LADE, Bt. (1759-1838) was born after his father's death in the hunting-field. In Mrs. Piozzi's *Anecdotes* it is reported that he asked, "Mr. Johnson, would you advise me to marry?" and received the reply, "I would advise no man to marry, Sir, who is not likely to propagate understanding." He married a notorious woman and squandered a great fortune. Written in 1780, the poem was first published in 1794, by Mrs. Piozzi.

Long-expected one and twenty
Ling'ring year at last is flown,
Pomp and Pleasure, Pride and Plenty
Great Sir John, are all your own.

5 Loosen'd from the Minor's tether,
Free to mortgage or to sell,
Wild as wind, and light as feather
Bid the slaves of thrift farewell.

Call the Bettys, Kates, and Jennys
10 Ev'ry name that laughs at Care,
Lavish of your Grandsire's guineas,
Show the Spirit of an heir.

>   All that prey on vice and folly
>   Joy to see their quarry fly,
> 15   Here the Gamester light and jolly
>   There the Lender grave and sly.
>
>   Wealth, Sir John, was made to wander,
>   Let it wander as it will;
>   See the Jocky, see the Pander,
> 20   Bid them come, and take their fill.
>
>   When the bonny Blade carouses,
>   Pockets full, and Spirits high,
>   What are acres? What are houses?
>   Only dirt, or wet or dry.
>
> 25   If the Guardian or the Mother
>   Tell the woes of wilful waste,
>   Scorn their counsel and their pother,
>   You can hang or drown at last.

21 *Blade:* "a brisk man, either fierce or gay, called so in contempt" (*Dictionary*).

On the Death of Dr. Robert Levet

DR. LEVET was a physician who had for many years occupied an apartment in Johnson's house. He was "an obscure practiser in physick among the lower people ... such was Johnson's predilection for him, and fanciful estimate of his moderate abilities, that I have heard him say he should not be satisfied, though attended by all the College of Physicians, unless he had Mr. Levet with him." (Boswell, *Life*, 1, 243.) He died on January 17, 1782 in his seventy-seventh year. Johnson wrote the poem shortly after Levet's death. It was published in *The Gentleman's Magazine*, August 1783.

ON THE DEATH OF DR. ROBERT LEVET

Condemn'd to hope's delusive mine,
    As on we toil from day to day,
By sudden blasts, or slow decline,
    Our social comforts drop away.

5 Well tried through many a varying year,
    See LEVET to the grave descend;
Officious, innocent, sincere,
    Of ev'ry friendless name the friend.

Yet still he fills affection's eye,
10   Obscurely wise, and coarsely kind;
Nor, letter'd arrogance, deny
    Thy praise to merit unrefin'd.

When fainting nature call'd for aid,
    And hov'ring death prepar'd the blow,
15 His vig'rous remedy display'd
    The power of art without the show.

In misery's darkest caverns known,
    His useful care was ever nigh,
Where hopeless anguish pour'd his groan,
20   And lonely want retir'd to die.

No summons mock'd by chill delay,
    No petty gain disdain'd by pride,
The modest wants of ev'ry day
    The toil of ev'ry day supplied.

7 *Officious:* obliging, dutiful.
12 *merit unrefin'd:* "Levet, madam, is a brutal fellow, but . . . his brutality is in his manners, not in his mind." Johnson, quoted in Boswell's *Life*, 1, 244.
19 With this line compare Pope's "Is it for thee the linnet pours his throat?" (*Essay on Man*), and Gray's "The Attic warbler pours her throat, Responsive to the cuckoo's note" ("On the Spring").

25 His virtues walk'd their narrow round,
      Nor made a pause, nor left a void;
    And sure th' Eternal Master found
      The single talent well employ'd.

    The busy day, the peaceful night,
30   Unfelt, uncounted, glided by;
    His frame was firm, his powers were bright,
      Tho' now his eightieth year was nigh.

    Then with no throbbing fiery pain,
      No cold gradations of decay,
35 Death broke at once the vital chain,
      And free'd his soul the nearest way.

Selected Poems of

OLIVER GOLDSMITH

edited by PETER DIXON

Acknowledgements

I am indebted to Dr. R. V. Johnson for checking some of the text; to Miss C. Cowan for advice about the notes; and to several of my former colleagues in Belfast for generous and expert help. Professor Leon Radzinowicz very kindly made available to me the information contained in the note to l. 318 of *The Deserted Village*. I owe a special debt to Miss Cilla Cromie and Miss Jean Sinclair, who have most patiently and painstakingly prepared the typescript.

P. DIXON

Contents

ACKNOWLEDGEMENTS	64
INTRODUCTION	66
GOLDSMITH'S LIFE	70
THE TEXT AND ITS ANNOTATION	72
THE POEMS	
The Gift	73
The Logicians Refuted	74
An Elegy on Mrs. Mary Blaize	76
The Double Transformation	77
A Description of an Author's Bedchamber	81
On the Death of the Right Honourable ★ ★ ★	82
The Traveller	84
Edwin and Angelina	102
An Elegy on the Death of a Mad Dog	108
Song: "When lovely woman stoops to folly"	109
Epilogue to *The Good Natur'd Man*	110
Epilogue to *The Sister*	112
The Deserted Village	114
Epitaph on Thomas Parnell	131
Song: "Ah me! when shall I marry me?"	131
Epilogue to *She Stoops to Conquer*	132
Epitaph on Edward Purdon	134
Retaliation	134
APPENDIXES	
A. *The Traveller*, ll. 381 ff.	143
B. *The Deserted Village*, ll. 43-6	144
SELECT BIBLIOGRAPHY	145

Introduction

DR. JOHNSON held the highest opinion of Goldsmith's literary abilities and the lowest of his intellectual power and resources. He told Boswell, emphatically, that "Goldsmith knows nothing; he has made up his mind about nothing". What may strike the modern reader is that Goldsmith had made up his mind about too few things; having elaborated a theory or turned a fine phrase, he was liable to repeat the good thing at every opportunity. Johnson himself complained that there was too much carry-over of material from *The Traveller* to *The Deserted Village*—it was one of the main reasons why he much preferred the earlier poem. Or again, exactly the same trick of witty anticlimax, which Goldsmith had picked up from a French song, is employed in two of his mock-elegies; it was clearly too neat a device to be used once and then discarded. Related to this is Goldsmith's sometimes slightly amusing reluctance to consign anything to the waste-paper basket. Writing to his brother Henry in January 1759 he encloses a few lines of a projected mock-heroic poem; a year later an expanded version of these lines ("A Description of an Author's Bed-chamber") figures in a farcical episode about a literary club in one of the "Chinese Letters"; and in 1770 some of its phrases turn up in the description of the inn in *The Deserted Village*. Similarly with the ballad *Edwin and Angelina*, which failed to win the attention and charity of the Countess of Northumberland, for whom it was privately printed. Unwilling to let the poem lie in obscurity, Goldsmith duly worked it into *The Vicar of Wakefield*, where it helps to strike a blow for simplicity against sophistication and luxury. Not all of this thrift and repetitiveness is to be put down simply to poverty of invention. Goldsmith spent much of his brief working life "scribbling" for publishers, making compilations and abridgments, turning out reviews and periodical essays. These things were done rapidly, under pressure, and Goldsmith soon learned to husband his resources.

Certainly he could never have been so splendidly lavish of intellect as Johnson. And as his was a less powerful, less "settled" mind, so it took more colour from its surroundings. Johnson's "imitations" of Juvenal bear the evident marks of his own personality; Goldsmith's imitation of Swift, "The Logicians Refuted", waited twenty-one years to be brought into the canon of his works, being in the meanwhile accepted and printed as authentic Swift. In theme and style it is a wonderfully clever copy. To mention only a single detail, the juxtaposition in l. 35 of judges, fiddlers, and dancing-masters is perfectly Swiftian—see, for example, the penultimate paragraph of *Gulliver's Travels*. Goldsmith was peculiarly attuned to the English Augustan age. He planned, about 1762, an edition of Pope's works; he wrote a sympathetic biography of Thomas Parnell; and he was content, on more than one occasion, to submerge his poetic personality in the authors of that age. "The Gift" is written in the off-hand style cultivated by Matthew Prior, while "The Double Transformation" imitates the same poet's light, colloquial verse-tales, though there is something of Swift in the sordid details of Flavia's beauty-preparations.

It was probably from Swift, too, that Goldsmith took the hint for the anapaestic couplets used so effectively in *Retaliation* (1774). He had previously, though not with the same sureness of touch, tried out this form in two epistles: *The Haunch of Venison* (written probably in 1771, published 1776), and a letter to Mrs. Bunbury (December 1773). These are relaxed performances, rather too comfortably verbose to find room in this selection, although at their best they skilfully capture the rhythms and tones of conversation. Their most notable passages are the mock-trial in the "Letter", and in *The Haunch of Venison* the arrival of the "Acquaintance, a Friend as he call'd himself", who makes off with the haunch, inviting the bewildered poet to eat it at *his* house, in very select company:

> Here, Porter—this venison with me to *Mile-end*;
> No stirring—I beg—my dear friend—my dear friend!
> Thus snatching his hat, he brusht off like the wind,
> And the porter and eatables follow'd behind.
>
> (ll. 55-8)

In *Retaliation*, too, geniality reigns: several of the epitaphs indulge in mild mockery only to end in neat compliment; nor does Goldsmith fail to glance at his own "compiling" (l. 88) and soft-heartedness (l. 16). The pace of the verse prevents the poem from becoming inappropriately solemn, while it allows the poet to make playful, though none the less telling, satiric thrusts: the portrait of Garrick, *acting* as an angel, is an acknowledged masterpiece.

In these three poems one comes nearest to Goldsmith the amiable companion, the man who, like Sir Joshua Reynolds, believed that most people in their leisure hours prefer amusement to instruction, and avoid company where their minds are kept at a stretch. It was with Reynolds that Goldsmith was most at home, while Johnson (and Boswell) frequently found his levity and nonsense simply irritating. But if Johnson could do no justice to this side of Goldsmith, he paid generous tribute to his unmistakably serious poetry. *The Traveller* he accounted the finest poem to appear since the death of Pope: any other reader would have put it second after Johnson's own *Vanity of Human Wishes*. In its ethical teaching, its firm structure, its survey of national manners, the poem has much in common with Johnson's masterpiece. It was almost inevitable that Johnson should help in revising it, though the exact amount of his assistance is not known. He told Reynolds that he had contributed eighteen lines; and several of the weightier cadences (e.g. ll. 279-80) seem to bear his stamp. Later, at Boswell's request, he marked only nine lines as certainly his, all but one from the strong concluding paragraph. That paragraph, indeed, slightly distorts the poem, imposing a Johnsonian dignity on Goldsmith's emotionalism. The first version ended with the pensive exile, harassed and terrified in the American wilds, who

> Casts a long look where England's glories shine,
> And bids his bosom sympathize with mine.
>
> (ll. 421-2)

We have come full circle; we are back with the homesick Traveller, who at the beginning of the poem cast his own long, fond looks towards the sanctities and securities of his brother's family life. Johnson's conclusion muffles the pathos, and asserts a more manly independence and fortitude than has so far been evident in the poem.

A similar complaint may be lodged against Johnson's contribution of four lines at the end of *The Deserted Village*. Their tone, in view of the plaintiveness and pessimism that have preceded them, seems over-assertive, a little over-confident. The impact of the poem depends much less on this kind of weighty Johnsonian statement than on Goldsmith's assault on our emotions, his alternating and contrasting of moods and situations. Indignation is set off against pity; the conviviality of the inn against the "solitary sports" of the usurping plutocrat; the varied murmur of the village against the monotonous calls of the lapwing. The emotional charge is further intensified by the frustration of the poet's hopes for peaceful retirement; he seeks refuge from care and grief in the "seats of [his] youth", only to find that the villagers themselves have fled, and with them the rural virtues. More than depopulation is at stake, and the poem is more than an elegy for Auburn. It is the disappearance of a whole way of life—"rural mirth and manners"— that Goldsmith laments, a way of life that has inevitably succumbed to the oppression of powerful wealth. Some eight years before the poem appeared Goldsmith described himself as being deeply moved by the fate of a village fifty miles from London, whose inhabitants had been expelled to make way for the private park and gardens of a wealthy City merchant.[1] And in the poem he denounces not, as has sometimes been hastily assumed, agricultural enclosures, but commercialism and the selfishness, extravagance, tyranny and corruption it brings in its train.[2] A merely "splendid" land has no use for "hospitable care", tenderness, innocence, piety, loyalty and love; in driving out these it drives out true happiness, even life itself. Goldsmith sees wealth and luxury in terms of poison and disease; the only "joy" they can offer is harsh and garish:

> Tumultuous grandeur crowds the blazing square,
> The rattling chariots clash, the torches glare.
>
> (ll. 321-2)

In actual historical fact, depopulation for the sake of private parks was a relatively rare occurrence, and villagers tended to move to industrial centres, drawn there by better wages, rather than to the colonies. But the force of Goldsmith's plea is not therefore diminished, since the plight of the village is for him symptomatic of a national decline. England, enfeebled by luxury, is near to moral ruin; Goldsmith is giving an impassioned warning to an affluent society.

The Deserted Village, eloquent and moving as it is, has become the poem by which Goldsmith is too entirely known, on which his poetical reputation is too exclusively based. I hope this selection will help to increase appreciation of the whole range of his poetical achievement. For Goldsmith, as Johnson's epitaph on him proclaims, touched every branch of literature, and adorned everything he touched.

P. DIXON

[1] See "The Revolution in Low Life" (1762), in *New Essays by Oliver Goldsmith*, ed. R. S. Crane (Chicago, 1927).

[2] See Appendix A below for Goldsmith's theory about commerce and tyranny; also the articles by H. J. Bell and Earl Miner in the Select Bibliography, section III.

Goldsmith's Life

1730(?)   Born at Pallas, County Longford, Ireland, on November 10. Family moved to village of Lissoy, County Westmeath.

1736-45   At various schools.

1745   Entered Trinity College, Dublin.

1750   Graduated B.A., after an unhappy college life. Began to read for Holy Orders. Took post as tutor.

1752   Began medical studies at Edinburgh.

1754   To Leyden (Holland) to continue studies.

1755   Left Leyden, and travelled on foot through France, Germany, Switzerland, Italy.

1756   Returned to England. Worked in London as an assistant in an apothecary's shop, and as a physician.

1757   Teaching. Book-reviewing for *The Monthly Review*.

1758   Appointed civilian physician with East India Company; the political situation in India prevented him from taking up the post.

1759   Reviewing for *The Critical Review;* writing essays for periodicals. *An Enquiry into the Present State of Polite Learning*.
October 6—November 24: *The Bee* (weekly magazine): Goldsmith was editor and virtually sole contributor.
First met Dr. Johnson.

1760-1   Reviewing. Editing *The Lady's Magazine*.
Periodical essays—especially the series of "Chinese Letters", which appeared (at first twice weekly) in *The Public Ledger*, January 24, 1760—August 14, 1761.

1761   First met Sir Joshua Reynolds.

1762   May 1: "Chinese Letters" published, with revisions, as *The Citizen of the World*.
The Life of Richard Nash.

1764	The Club, an intimate literary society, formed; the nine charter members included Johnson, Reynolds, Burke and Goldsmith. December 19: *The Traveller*.
1765	Resumed, very briefly, his practice as a physician.
1766	March 27: *The Vicar of Wakefield*.
1768	January 29: First performance of *The Good Natur'd Man*. May: Death of his brother Henry.
1770	May 26: *The Deserted Village*. July: Travelled on the Continent with the Horneck family.
1773	March 15: First performance of *She Stoops to Conquer*. Health breaking down; periods of depression.
1774	Goldsmith died, on April 4. Posthumous publications: *Retaliation* (April 19); *An History of the Earth, and Animated Nature* (July 1).

The Text and its Annotation

A NOTE prefixed to each poem gives the date of publication, and something of the background of the poem; it also indicates briefly the source of the text that follows. Unless otherwise stated this text reproduces, with the exceptions mentioned below, that of the poem's first printing. Where Goldsmith revised a work for later editions I have assembled an eclectic text, based on the first edition, and modified only by those readings from revised editions which would appear to have Goldsmith's authority. In all such cases I have simply listed in the head-note those later editions upon which I have drawn: the reader is referred to Professor Friedman's forthcoming Clarendon Press edition for a full account of Goldsmith's often very happy second thoughts.

I have kept editorial interference to a minimum. The sole verbal emendation (*Deserted Village*, l. 69), and two important changes in punctuation ("On the Death of the Right Honourable★★★", ll. 17-18; *Edwin and Angelina*, l. 93) are recorded in the notes. Some minor modifications of the original punctuation have been made where I felt that the sense might not be perfectly clear to the modern reader; these are not recorded. I have also silently corrected a few misprints, and supplied apostrophes and question-marks when the sense required them; in *Edwin and Angelina* I have used modern conventions for the presentation of direct speech.

The Notes:

Where Goldsmith may have intended a word to carry more than one sense or shade of meaning, I have for convenience distinguished the senses as (1), (2), etc.

All quotations from Dr. Johnson's *Dictionary of the English Language* are from the fourth edition, 2 vols., London, 1773.

The Gift

To IRIS, in Bow-Street, Covent-Garden

THIS light-hearted piece, freely adapted from a French original, was first printed in Goldsmith's short-lived periodical, *The Bee*, on October 13, 1759. The text is from the collected edition of the *Bee* essays, published at the end of the same year.

    Say, cruel IRIS, pretty rake,
        Dear mercenary beauty,
    What annual offering shall I make,
        Expressive of my duty?

5   My heart, a victim to thine eyes,
        Should I at once deliver,
    Say, would the angry fair one prize
        The gift, who slights the giver?

    A bill, a jewel, watch, or toy,
10   My rivals give—and let 'em.
    If gems, or gold, impart a joy,
        I'll give them—when I get 'em.

    I'll give—but not the full-blown rose,
        Or rose-bud more in fashion;
15 Such short-liv'd offerings but disclose
        A transitory passion.

    I'll give thee something yet unpaid,
        Not less sincere, than civil:
    I'll give thee—Ah! too charming maid;
20   I'll give thee—To the Devil.

1 *rake:* here, "an immoral woman, a prostitute".
9 *bill:* the eighteenth-century counterpart of the modern cheque. *toy:* trinket.

The Logicians Refuted

This poem appeared in *The Busy Body* (a weekly magazine), on October 18, 1759, with an introductory note stating that it had been written by Swift and presented to the magazine "by a Nobleman of distinguished Learning and Taste". It was first printed as Goldsmith's in 1780.

> Logicians have but ill defin'd
> As rational, the human kind;
> Reason, they say, belongs to man,
> But let them prove it if they can.
> 5 Wise Aristotle and Smiglesius,
> By ratiocinations specious,
> Have strove to prove with great precision,
> With definition and division,
> *Homo est ratione preditum*;
> 10 But for my soul I cannot credit 'em;
> And must in spite of them maintain,
> That man and all his ways are vain;
> And that this boasted lord of nature,
> Is both a weak and erring creature;
> 15 That instinct is a surer guide
> Than reason-boasting mortals' pride;
> And that brute beasts are far before 'em,
> *Deus est anima brutorum.*
> Whoever knew an honest brute,
> 20 At law his neighbour prosecute,
> Bring action for assault and battery,
> Or friend beguile with lies and flattery?

5 *Smiglesius:* a Polish Jesuit, theologian and logician. In the *Life of Parnell* Goldsmith refers to his "dreary subtleties".

6 i.e. by reasoning that appears sound but is really fallacious.

9 i.e. man is endowed with reason.

18 i.e. God is the soul of beasts (the instincts of animals are implanted, and guided, by Providence).

O'er plains they ramble unconfin'd,
No politics disturb their mind;
25 They eat their meals, and take their sport,
Nor know who's in or out at court.
They never to the levee go
To treat as dearest friend, a foe:
They never importune his grace,
30 Nor ever cringe to men in place;
Nor undertake a dirty job,
Nor draw the quill to write for B—b.
Fraught with invective they ne'er go,
To folks at Pater-Noster-Row:
35 No judges, fidlers, dancing-masters,
No pick-pockets, or poetasters,
Are known to honest quadrupeeds,
No single brute his fellows leads.
Brutes never meet in bloody fray,
40 Nor cut each other's throats for pay.
Of beasts, it is confess'd, the ape
Comes nearest us in human shape,
Like man he imitates each fashion,
And malice is his ruling passion:
45 But both in malice and grimaces,
A courtier any ape surpasses.
Behold him humbly cringing wait,
Upon the minister of state:

26 *in or out:* i.e. of office and favour.

27 *levee:* a morning reception, held at Court, or at a nobleman's house.

30 *cringe:* bow obsequiously.

31 The word *job* had unsavoury associations in the eighteenth century. Johnson defined it as "a low mean lucrative busy affair".

32 *quill* (quill-pen) was often used sarcastically by Pope, Swift, etc., to suggest venomous and cheap writing.   B[o]b: Sir Robert Walpole, Prime Minister 1715-17 and 1721-42; his Ministry was defended by many hired political journalists.

34 i.e. to publishers—many of whom, including the publisher of *The Busy Body*, had premises in this street in the City of London. Goldsmith's first and unhappiest period as a book-reviewer was spent there.

>   View him soon after to inferiors
> 50 Aping the conduct of superiors:
>   He promises with equal air,
>   And to perform takes equal care.
>   He in his turn finds imitators,
>   At court the porters, lacquees, waiters,
> 55 Their master's manners still contract,
>   And footmen, lords and dukes can act.
>   Thus at the court, both great and small
>   Behave alike, for all ape all.

55 *contract:* catch, like a disease.

An Elegy on that Glory of Her Sex Mrs. Mary Blaize

THIS mock-elegy, modelled on a popular French song, appeared in *The Bee* on October 27, 1759. Goldsmith despised the flattering, and often bombastic, elegies that were then in vogue. The text given here is that of the collected volume of *Bee* essays, issued in December 1759.

>   Good people all, with one accord,
>   Lament for Madam BLAIZE,
>   Who never wanted a good word—
>   *From those who spoke her praise.*
>
> 5   The needy seldom pass'd her door,
>   And always found her kind;
>   She freely lent to all the poor,—
>   *Who left a pledge behind.*
>
>   She strove the neighbourhood to please,
> 10   With manners wond'rous winning,
>   And never follow'd wicked ways,—
>   *Unless when she was sinning.*

8 i.e. she was a pawn-broker.

At church, in silks and sattins new,
   With hoop of monstrous size,
15 She never slumber'd in her pew,—
   But when she shut her eyes.

Her love was sought, I do aver,
   By twenty beaus and more;
The king himself has follow'd her,—
20 *When she has walk'd before.*

But now her wealth and finery fled,
   Her hangers-on cut short all;
The doctors found, when she was dead,—
   Her last disorder mortal.

25 Let us lament, in sorrow sore,
   For Kent-street well may say,
That had she liv'd a twelve-month more,—
   She had not dy'd to-day.

26 *Kent-street:* a poor neighbourhood in Southwark, London.

The Double Transformation

A TALE

UNDER the title "The Double Metamorphosis" this tale was published in *The Weekly Magazine: or, Gentleman and Lady's Polite Companion* on January 5, 1760. It was later included, in a modified form, in *Essays: By Mr. Goldsmith* (London, 1765), and was again revised, in order to increase the pace of the narrative, for the second edition of the *Essays* in the following year.

The *Weekly Magazine* text is reprinted by W. D. Paden and C. K. Hyder in *A Concordance to the Poems of Oliver Goldsmith* (Lawrence, Kansas, 1940), pp. xi-xii. The text here is based on this reprint, but incorporates the revisions of 1765 and 1766.

Secluded from domestic strife
   Jack Book-worm led a college life;
   A fellowship at twenty five
   Made him the happiest man alive,
5 He drank his glass, and crack'd his joke,
   And Freshmen wonder'd as he spoke.

   Such pleasures unallay'd with care,
   Could any accident impair?
   Could Cupid's shaft at length transfix,
10 Our swain arriv'd at thirty six?
   O had the archer ne'er come down
   To ravage in a country town!
   Or Flavia been content to stop,
   At triumphs in a Fleet-street shop.
15 O had her eyes forgot to blaze!
   Or Jack had wanted eyes to gaze.
   O—but let exclamation cease,
   Her presence banish'd all his peace.
   So with decorum all things carry'd;
20 Miss frown'd, and blush'd, and then was married.

   Need we expose to vulgar sight,
   The raptures of the bridal night?
   Need we intrude on hallow'd ground,
   Or draw the curtains clos'd around?
25 Let it suffice, that each had charms;
   He clasp'd a goddess in his arms;
   And tho' she felt his usage rough,
   Yet in a man 'twas well enough.

   The honey-moon like lightening flew,
30 The second brought its transports too.
   A third, a fourth were not amiss,
   The fifth was friendship mix'd with bliss:
   But when a twelvemonth pass'd away
   Jack found his goddess made of clay:

29 *honey-moon:* the first month after marriage.

35   Found half the charms that deck'd her face,
      Arose from powder, shreds, or lace;
      But still the worst remain'd behind,
      That very face had robb'd her mind.

      Skill'd in no other arts was she,
40   But dressing, patching, repartee;
      And just as humour rose or fell,
      By turns a slattern or a belle:
      'Tis true she dress'd with modern grace,
      Half naked at a ball or race;
45   But when at home, at board or bed,
      Five greasy nightcaps wrap'd her head.
      Could so much beauty condescend,
      To be a dull domestic friend?
      Could any curtain-lectures bring
50   To decency so fine a thing?
      In short by night 'twas fits or fretting,
      By day 'twas gadding or coquetting.
      Fond to be seen she kept a bevy
      Of powder'd coxcombs at her levy;
55   The squire and captain took their stations,
      And twenty other near relations;
      Jack suck'd his pipe and often broke
      A sigh in suffocating smoke;
      While all their hours were pass'd between
60   Insulting repartee or spleen.

      Thus as her faults each day were known,
      He thinks her features coarser grown;
      He fancies every vice she shews
      Or thins her lip, or points her nose:

36 *shreds:* lengths of gold or silver thread.
  49 *curtain-lecture:* "a reproof given by a wife to her husband in bed" (Johnson's *Dictionary*). Goldsmith appropriately reverses the rôles.
  54 *levy:* (more commonly *levee*) a reception of visitors held on rising from bed; a morning assembly.

65 Whenever rage or envy rise,
    How wide her mouth, how wild her eyes!
    He knows not how, but so it is,
    Her face is grown a knowing phyz;
    And tho' her fops are wondrous civil,
70 He thinks her ugly as the Devil.

    Now, to perplex the ravell'd nooze,
    As each a different way pursues,
    While sullen or loquacious strife
    Promis'd to hold them on for life,
75 That dire disease whose ruthless power
    Withers the beauty's transient flower:
    Lo! the small pox whose horrid glare,
    Levell'd its terrors at the fair;
    And rifling ev'ry youthful grace,
80 Left but the remnant of a face.

    The glass grown hateful to her sight,
    Reflected now a perfect fright:
    Each former art she vainly tries
    To bring back lustre to her eyes.
85 In vain she tries her pastes and creams,
    To smooth her skin, or hide its seams;
    Her country beaux and city cousins,
    Lovers no more, flew off by dozens:
    The squire himself was seen to yield,
90 And even the captain quit the field.

    Poor Madam now condemn'd to hack
    The rest of life with anxious Jack,
    Perceiving others fairly flown
    Attempted pleasing him alone.

68 *knowing:* cunning, shrewd.   *phyz:* face, expression—a colloquial, and derogatory, abbreviation of *physiognomy*.

71 *nooze:* (*noose*) the marriage knot (with a hint, in this context, of the hangman's).

78 *Levell'd:* aimed, directed.

91 *to hack:* to plod along.

95 Jack soon was dazzl'd to behold
    Her present face surpass the old;
    With modesty her cheeks are dy'd,
    Humility displaces pride;
    For tawdry finery is seen
100 A person ever neatly clean:
    No more presuming on her sway
    She learns good nature every day,
    Serenely gay, and strict in duty,
    Jack finds his wife a perfect beauty.

A Description of an Author's Bedchamber

FOR the history of these lines see the Introduction to this edition, p. 66. They were first published on May 2, 1760, in one of the "Chinese Letters" that Goldsmith contributed to *The Public Ledger* and later collected, revised, and republished as *The Citizen of the World* (London, 1762). The Chinese Philosopher hears the lines read to "a club of authors" by an impecunious poet; they are the opening of his new epic poem. The text here is that of the first edition of *The Citizen of the World*.

    Where the Red Lion flaring o'er the way,
    Invites each passing stranger that can pay;
    Where Calvert's butt, and Parsons' black champaign,
    Regale the drabs and bloods of Drury lane;
5   There in a lonely room, from bailiffs snug,
    The muse found Scroggen stretch'd beneath a rug.
    A window patch'd with paper lent a ray,
    That dimly shew'd the state in which he lay;
    The sanded floor that grits beneath the tread;
10 The humid wall with paltry pictures spread:

3 Parsons and the Calvert family were brewers of porter, a dark and bitter beer also known as "entire butt beer" and "black champagne".

4 During the eighteenth century Drury Lane was a haunt of prostitutes (*drabs*), and rakes (*bloods*).

The royal game of goose was there in view,
  And the twelve rules the royal martyr drew;
  The seasons fram'd with listing found a place,
  And brave prince William shew'd his lamp-black face:
15 The morn was cold, he views with keen desire
  The rusty grate unconscious of a fire:
  With beer and milk arrears the frieze was scor'd,
  And five crack'd tea cups dress'd the chimney board.
  A night-cap deck'd his brows instead of bay,
20 A cap by night—a stocking all the day!

11 *royal game of goose:* a game played with board and dice, rather like "Snakes and Ladders".

12 *twelve rules:* twelve homely maxims, said to have been found in Charles I's study. A printed sheet, containing these "rules" and a woodcut of Charles's execution, made a popular (and cheap) wall decoration.

13 *seasons:* prints of "The Four Seasons" were also popular.   *listing:* the border or selvage of a piece of cloth.

14 *prince William:* William Augustus, Duke of Cumberland, third son of George II, hero of the battle of Culloden (1745). The portrait is presumably a silhouette.

16 *unconscious* (i.e. "unaware of" and hence simply "without" a fire) has a neat mock-heroic effect. The word *conscious*, used (with a hint of its Latin meaning) in the sense of "privy to a secret", was a favourite bit of eighteenth-century poetic diction.

17 *frieze:* the vertical part of a mantelpiece, between the grate and the mantelshelf.

19 *bay:* In classical times crowns or garlands of bay-leaves were given to the most distinguished poets.

On the Death of the Right Honourable * * *

THIS piece, like the preceding one, was first printed in the "Chinese Letters"—on March 4, 1761. The Chinese Philosopher confesses his amazement "that none have yet found out the secret of flattering the worthless, and yet of preserving a safe conscience", and encloses the following elegy, "in which the flattery is perfectly fine, and yet the poet perfectly innocent". The text is that of the first edition of *The Citizen of the World*.

> Ye muses, pour the pitying tear
> For Pollio snatch'd away:
> O had he liv'd another year!
> —*He had not dy'd to-day.*
>
> 5 O, were he born to bless mankind,
> In virtuous times of yore,
> Heroes themselves had fallen behind!
> —*Whene'er he went before.*
>
> How sad the groves and plains appear,
> 10 And sympathetic sheep;
> Even pitying hills would drop a tear!
> —*If hills could learn to weep.*
>
> His bounty in exalted strain
> Each bard might well display:
> 15 Since none implor'd relief in vain!
> —*That went reliev'd away.*
>
> And hark! I hear the tuneful throng
> His obsequies forbid;
> He still shall live, shall live as long
> 20 —*As ever dead man did.*

2 The Roman Consul *Pollio* was a generous patron of Virgil and Horace.

17-18 The Chinese Philosopher, introducing the elegy, observes that on the death of a great man, when the undertaker "has soberly laid the body in the grave", the poet "is ready to fix it figuratively among the stars". The elegiac poets (*tuneful throng*) "forbid" funeral rites and lamentations for Pollio because he is assured of immortality.

The first edition reads: "And hark! I hear the tuneful throng;/His obsequies forbid/He still shall live, . . ." This punctuation is unintelligible, and breaks the rhythmical pattern established in the preceding stanzas.

The Traveller

THE poem was begun in 1755-6, when Goldsmith was travelling on foot through the countries he describes. Under the title *A Prospect of Society* it was ready for the press in 1764; publication was held up, however, by a serious blunder in the printing-house, and Goldsmith took the opportunity to revise and expand the text, with Dr. Johnson's assistance, and to change the title. *The Traveller* eventually appeared on December 19, 1764. It was an immediate success, and established its author as an important poet. The text below embodies the revisions that Goldsmith made for the second and sixth editions (1765 and 1770).

TO THE REV. HENRY GOLDSMITH

DEAR SIR,

I am sensible that the friendship between us can acquire no new force from the ceremonies of a Dedication; and perhaps it demands an excuse thus to prefix your name to my attempts, which you decline giving with your own. But as a part of this
5 Poem was formerly written to you from Switzerland, the whole can now, with propriety, be only inscribed to you. It will also throw a light upon many parts of it, when the reader understands that it is addressed to a man, who, despising Fame and Fortune, has retired early to Happiness and Obscurity,
10 with an income of forty pounds a year.

I now perceive, my dear brother, the wisdom of your humble choice. You have entered upon a sacred office, where the harvest is great, and the labourers are but few; while you have left the field of Ambition, where the labourers are many,
15 and the harvest not worth carrying away. But of all kinds of ambition, what from the refinement of the times, from differing systems of criticism, and from the divisions of party, that which pursues poetical fame is the wildest.

8-10 Henry Goldsmith, the poet's elder brother, was curate at Pallas, Oliver's birthplace.

16 *what from:* on account of ...

17 *party* (also **35**): political faction.

Poetry makes a principal amusement among unpolished nations; but in a country verging to the extremes of refinement, Painting and Music come in for a share. As these offer the feeble mind a less laborious entertainment, they at first rival Poetry, and at length supplant her; they engross all that favour once shewn to her, and though but younger sisters, seize upon the elder's birth-right.

Yet, however this art may be neglected by the powerful, it is still in greater danger from the mistaken efforts of the learned to improve it. What criticisms have we not heard of late in favour of blank verse, and Pindaric odes, chorusses, anapests and iambics, alliterative care, and happy negligence. Every absurdity has now a champion to defend it, and as he is generally much in the wrong, so he has always much to say; for error is ever talkative.

But there is an enemy to this art still more dangerous, I mean party. Party entirely distorts the judgment, and destroys the taste. When the mind is once infected with this disease, it can only find pleasure in what contributes to encrease the distemper. Like the tyger, that seldom desists from pursuing man after having once preyed upon human flesh, the reader, who has once gratified his appetite with calumny, makes, ever after, the most agreeable feast upon murdered reputation. Such readers generally admire some half-witted thing, who wants to be thought a bold man, having lost the character of a wise one. Him they dignify with the name of poet; his tawdry lampoons are called satires, his turbulence is said to be force, and his phrenzy fire.

What reception a Poem may find, which has neither abuse, party, nor blank verse to support it, I cannot tell, nor am I solicitous to know. My aims are right. Without espousing

29 In his *Enquiry into the Present State of Polite Learning* (1759) Goldsmith had commented on the abuse of blank verse: "Nothing but the greatest sublimity of subject can render such a measure pleasing; however, we now see it used upon the most trivial occasions."

44 *poet:* Goldsmith is probably referring to Charles Churchill (1731-64), notorious for his hard-hitting personal satires.

50 the cause of any party, I have attempted to moderate the rage of all. I have endeavoured to shew, that there may be equal happiness in states, that are differently governed from our own; that every state has a particular principle of happiness, and that this principle in each may be carried to a mischievous
55 excess. There are few can judge, better than yourself, how far these positions are illustrated in this Poem.

I am, dear Sir,
Your most affectionate Brother,
OLIVER GOLDSMITH.

The Traveller, or a Prospect of Society

    Remote, unfriended, melancholy, slow,
Or by the lazy Scheld, or wandering Po;
Or onward, where the rude Carinthian boor
Against the houseless stranger shuts the door;
5 Or where Campania's plain forsaken lies,
A weary waste expanding to the skies:
Where'er I roam, whatever realms to see,
My heart untravell'd fondly turns to thee;
Still to my brother turns, with ceaseless pain,
10 And drags at each remove a lengthening chain.

    Eternal blessings crown my earliest friend,
And round his dwelling guardian saints attend;
Blest be that spot, where chearful guests retire
To pause from toil, and trim their evening fire;
15 Blest that abode, where want and pain repair,

Title of poem: *Prospect* = view.

  3 *Carinthian boor:* Carinthia, a mountainous district in S. Austria, was noted for inhospitality.

  5 *Campania's plain:* the Campagna of Rome, a plain south of that city; in the eighteenth century it was still swampy and malarial.

  6 *expanding to the skies:* stretching to the horizon.

And every stranger finds a ready chair;
Blest be those feasts with simple plenty crown'd,
Where all the ruddy family around
Laugh at the jests or pranks that never fail,
20 Or sigh with pity at some mournful tale,
Or press the bashful stranger to his food,
And learn the luxury of doing good.

But me, not destin'd such delights to share,
My prime of life in wand'ring spent and care:
25 Impell'd, with steps unceasing, to pursue
Some fleeting good, that mocks me with the view;
That, like the circle bounding earth and skies,
Allures from far, yet, as I follow, flies;
My fortune leads to traverse realms alone,
30 And find no spot of all the world my own.

Even now, where Alpine solitudes ascend
I sit me down a pensive hour to spend;
And, plac'd on high above the storm's career,
Look downward where an hundred realms appear;
35 Lakes, forests, cities, plains extending wide,
The pomp of kings, the shepherd's humbler pride.

When thus Creation's charms around combine,
Amidst the store, should thankless pride repine?
Say, should the philosophic mind disdain
40 That good, which makes each humbler bosom vain?
Let school-taught pride dissemble all it can,
These little things are great to little man;
And wiser he, whose sympathetic mind
Exults in all the good of all mankind.
45 Ye glittering towns, with wealth and splendour crown'd,
Ye fields, where summer spreads profusion round,

29 *leads:* the object of this verb is *me* in l. 23.
41 *school-taught:* the reference is to "schools" of philosophy, especially that of the Stoics.

Ye lakes, whose vessels catch the busy gale,
Ye bending swains, that dress the flow'ry vale,
For me your tributary stores combine;
50 Creation's heir, the world, the world is mine.

As some lone miser visiting his store,
Bends at his treasure, counts, recounts it o'er;
Hoards after hoards his rising raptures fill,
Yet still he sighs, for hoards are wanting still:
55 Thus to my breast alternate passions rise,
Pleas'd with each good that heaven to man supplies:
Yet oft a sigh prevails, and sorrows fall,
To see the hoard of human bliss so small;
And oft I wish, amidst the scene, to find
60 Some spot to real happiness consign'd,
Where my worn soul, each wand'ring hope at rest,
May gather bliss to see my fellows blest.

But where to find that happiest spot below,
Who can direct, when all pretend to know?
65 The shudd'ring tenant of the frigid zone
Boldly proclaims that happiest spot his own,
Extols the treasures of his stormy seas,
And his long nights of revelry and ease;
The naked negroe, panting at the line,
70 Boasts of his golden sands and palmy wine,
Basks in the glare, or stems the tepid wave,
And thanks his Gods for all the good they gave.
Such is the patriot's boast, where'er we roam,
His first best country ever is at home.
75 And yet, perhaps, if countries we compare,
And estimate the blessings which they share;

---

47 *gale* (also 121, 139): "a wind not tempestuous, yet stronger than a breeze" (Johnson's *Dictionary*).
69 *line:* the Equator.
70 *palmy:* made from the sap of palm-trees.

Tho' patriots flatter, still shall wisdom find
An equal portion dealt to all mankind,
As different good, by Art or Nature given,
80 To different nations makes their blessings even.

Nature, a mother kind alike to all,
Still grants her bliss at Labour's earnest call;
With food as well the peasant is supply'd
On Idra's cliffs as Arno's shelvy side;
85 And though the rocky crested summits frown,
These rocks, by custom, turn to beds of down.

From Art more various are the blessings sent;
Wealth, commerce, honor, liberty, content:
Yet these each other's power so strong contest,
90 That either seems destructive of the rest.
Where wealth and freedom reign contentment fails,
And honour sinks where commerce long prevails.
Hence every state, to one lov'd blessing prone,
Conforms and models life to that alone.
95 Each to the favourite happiness attends,
And spurns the plan that aims at other ends;
'Till, carried to excess in each domain,
This favourite good begets peculiar pain.

But let us try these truths with closer eyes,
100 And trace them through the prospect as it lies:
Here for a while my proper cares resign'd,
Here let me sit in sorrow for mankind,
Like yon neglected shrub, at random cast,
That shades the steep, and sighs at every blast.

84 *Idra:* Idrija (N. Yugoslavia), a town famous for its quicksilver mines. The barren cliffs, yielding mineral riches, are contrasted with the fertile slopes of the valley of the Arno, in Tuscany.
98 *peculiar pain:* its own special pain.
99 *try:* test, examine.
101 *my proper cares:* my own cares.

105   Far to the right, where Appennine ascends,
        Bright as the summer, Italy extends;
        Its uplands sloping deck the mountain's side,
        Woods over woods, in gay theatric pride;
        While oft some temple's mould'ring tops between,
110   With venerable grandeur mark the scene.

        Could Nature's bounty satisfy the breast,
        The sons of Italy were surely blest.
        Whatever fruits in different climes are found,
        That proudly rise or humbly court the ground;
115   Whatever blooms in torrid tracts appear,
        Whose bright succession decks the varied year;
        Whatever sweets salute the northern sky
        With vernal lives that blossom but to die;
        These here disporting, own the kindred soil,
120   Nor ask luxuriance from the planter's toil;
        While sea-born gales their gelid wings expand
        To winnow fragrance round the smiling land.

        But small the bliss that sense alone bestows,
        And sensual bliss is all the nation knows.
125   In florid beauty groves and fields appear,
        Man seems the only growth that dwindles here.
        Contrasted faults through all his manners reign,
        Though poor, luxurious, though submissive, vain,
        Though grave, yet trifling, zealous, yet untrue,
130   And even in penance planning sins anew.
        All evils here contaminate the mind,
        That opulence departed leaves behind;
        For wealth was theirs, nor far remov'd the date,
        When commerce proudly flourish'd through the state:

   108 *theatric:* (1) resembling a theatre or amphitheatre in formation; and (2) "stagey", showy.

   119 *own:* acknowledge. The gay and profuse growth of the plants shows that the soil is congenial.

   121 *gelid:* cooling, refreshingly cold.

   122 *winnow:* waft, scatter.

135 At her command the palace learnt to rise,
    Again the long-fall'n column sought the skies;
    The canvass glow'd beyond even Nature warm,
    The pregnant quarry teem'd with human form.
    Till, more unsteady than the southern gale,
140 Commerce on other shores display'd her sail;
    While nought remain'd of all that riches gave,
    But towns unman'd, and lords without a slave:
    And late the nation found, with fruitless skill,
    Its former strength was but plethoric ill.

145   Yet, still the loss of wealth is here supplied
    By arts, the splendid wrecks of former pride;
    From these the feeble heart and long fall'n mind
    An easy compensation seem to find.
    Here may be seen, in bloodless pomp array'd,
150 The paste-board triumph and the cavalcade;
    Processions form'd for piety and love,
    A mistress or a saint in every grove.
    By sports like these are all their cares beguil'd,
    The sports of children satisfy the child;
155 Each nobler aim represt by long controul,
    Now sinks at last, or feebly mans the soul;
    While low delights, succeeding fast behind,
    In happier meanness occupy the mind:
    As in those domes, where Cæsars once bore sway,
160 Defac'd by time and tottering in decay,

135-8 These lines very successfully convey the vigour and splendour of the Italian Renaissance—the classical revival in architecture, the abundant vitality of painting, the countless statues carved from the quarried marble.

139-40 With the discovery of America, and of the sea-routes to India, commercial leadership passed from the North Italian ports.

142 *unman'd:* depopulated.

144 *plethoric ill:* a morbid condition, thought to be caused by overfulness of blood; more generally, any unhealthy repletion or excess. (Cf. *Deserted Village*, ll. 389 ff.)

150 Pageants and processions with floats and fancy-dress costumes.

159 *domes:* palaces.

There in the ruin, heedless of the dead,
The shelter-seeking peasant builds his shed,
And, wond'ring man could want the larger pile,
Exults, and owns his cottage with a smile.

165   My soul turn from them, turn we to survey
Where rougher climes a nobler race display,
Where the bleak Swiss their stormy mansions tread,
And force a churlish soil for scanty bread;
No product here the barren hills afford,
170 But man and steel, the soldier and his sword.
No vernal blooms their torpid rocks array,
But winter lingering chills the lap of May;
No Zephyr fondly sues the mountain's breast,
But meteors glare, and stormy glooms invest.

175   Yet still, even here, content can spread a charm,
Redress the clime, and all its rage disarm.
Though poor the peasant's hut, his feasts though small,
He sees his little lot, the lot of all;
Sees no contiguous palace rear its head
180 To shame the meanness of his humble shed;
No costly lord the sumptuous banquet deal
To make him loath his vegetable meal;
But calm, and bred in ignorance and toil,
Each wish contracting, fits him to the soil.
185 Chearful at morn he wakes from short repose,
Breasts the keen air, and carrols as he goes;
With patient angle trolls the finny deep,
Or drives his vent'rous plow-share to the steep;
190 And drags the struggling savage into day.
Or seeks the den where snow tracks mark the way,

  167 *mansions:* the places or regions where they live; their homeland.
  170 Swiss mercenary soldiers were renowned for their prowess.
  171 *torpid:* unproductive. **173** *sues:* woos. **179** *contiguous:* neighbouring.
  187 *angle:* fishing-tackle. To *troll* is to fish (usually for pike) with a running line.
  189-90 Bear-hunting. In his *History of the Earth* Goldsmith describes the

At night returning, every labour sped,
He sits him down the monarch of a shed;
Smiles by his chearful fire, and round surveys
His children's looks, that brighten at the blaze:
195 While his lov'd partner, boastful of her hoard,
Displays her cleanly platter on the board;
And haply too some pilgrim, thither led,
With many a tale repays the nightly bed.

    Thus every good his native wilds impart,
200 Imprints the patriot passion on his heart,
And even those ills, that round his mansion rise,
Enhance the bliss his scanty fund supplies.
Dear is that shed to which his soul conforms,
And dear that hill which lifts him to the storms;
205 And as a child, when scaring sounds molest,
Clings close and closer to the mother's breast;
So the loud torrent, and the whirlwind's roar,
But bind him to his native mountains more.

    Such are the charms to barren states assign'd;
210 Their wants but few, their wishes all confin'd.
Yet let them only share the praises due,
If few their wants, their pleasures are but few;
For every want, that stimulates the breast,
Becomes a source of pleasure when redrest.
215 Whence from such lands each pleasing science flies,
That first excites desire, and then supplies;
Unknown to them, when sensual pleasures cloy,
To fill the languid pause with finer joy;
Unknown those powers that raise the soul to flame,
220 Catch every nerve, and vibrate through the frame.
Their level life is but a smould'ring fire,
Unquench'd by want, unfann'd by strong desire;

brown bear of the Alps as savage and solitary: "The natives in those countries where it is found, hunt it with great perseverance and alacrity."
   215 *science:* "any art or species of knowledge" (Johnson's *Dictionary*).
   216 *supplies:* satisfies the desire it has first excited.

        Unfit for raptures, or, if raptures cheer
        On some high festival of once a year,
225 In wild excess the vulgar breast takes fire,
        Till, buried in debauch, the bliss expire.

        But not their joys alone thus coarsly flow:
        Their morals, like their pleasures, are but low.
        For, as refinement stops, from sire to son
230 Unalter'd, unimprov'd the manners run,
        And love's and friendship's finely pointed dart
        Fall blunted from each indurated heart.
        Some sterner virtues o'er the mountain's breast
        May sit, like falcons cow'ring on the nest;
235 But all the gentler morals, such as play
        Through life's more cultur'd walks, and charm the way,
        These far dispers'd, on timorous pinions fly,
        To sport and flutter in a kinder sky.

        To kinder skies, where gentler manners reign,
240 I turn; and France displays her bright domain.
        Gay sprightly land of mirth and social ease,
        Pleas'd with thyself, whom all the world can please,
        How often have I led thy sportive choir,
        With tuneless pipe, beside the murmuring Loire?
245 Where shading elms along the margin grew,
        And freshen'd from the wave the Zephyr flew;
        And haply, tho' my harsh touch faltering still,
        But mock'd all tune, and marr'd the dancer's skill;
        Yet would the village praise my wond'rous power,
250 And dance, forgetful of the noon-tide hour.
        Alike all ages. Dames of ancient days

  230-2 In *A Prospect of Society* the equivalent of l. 230 is "Manners in one unending track will run"; so that *Fall* in l. 232 was also originally future tense. When he revised the earlier line Goldsmith omitted to change *Fall* to *Falls*.

  232 *indurated:* hardened, unfeeling.

  234 *cow'ring:* crouching.

Have led their children through the mirthful maze,
And the gay grandsire, skill'd in gestic lore,
Has frisk'd beneath the burthen of threescore.

255   So blest a life these thoughtless realms display,
Thus idly busy rolls their world away:
Theirs are those arts that mind to mind endear,
For honour forms the social temper here.
Honour, that praise which real merit gains,
260   Or even imaginary worth obtains,
Here passes current; paid from hand to hand,
It shifts in splendid traffic round the land:
From courts to camps, to cottages it strays,
And all are taught an avarice of praise;
265   They please, are pleas'd, they give to get esteem,
Till, seeming blest, they grow to what they seem.

But while this softer art their bliss supplies,
It gives their follies also room to rise;
For praise too dearly lov'd, or warmly sought,
270   Enfeebles all internal strength of thought,
And the weak soul, within itself unblest,
Leans for all pleasure on another's breast.
Hence ostentation here, with tawdry art,
Pants for the vulgar praise which fools impart;
275   Here vanity assumes her pert grimace,
And trims her robes of frize with copper lace,
Here beggar pride defrauds her daily cheer,
To boast one splendid banquet once a year;
The mind still turns where shifting fashion draws,
280   Nor weighs the solid worth of self applause.

253 *gestic lore:* traditional dance-steps and figures.
258 *social temper:* the social "climate".
262 *traffic:* trade, commercial transactions: the word was often used, as here, with a pejorative sense.
276 *frize:* (frieze) a coarse woollen cloth.   *copper lace:* imitation gold or silver lace.
279 *still:* continually.

> To men of other minds my fancy flies,
> Embosom'd in the deep where Holland lies;
> Methinks her patient sons before me stand,
> Where the broad ocean leans against the land,
> 285 And, sedulous to stop the coming tide,
> Lift the tall rampire's artificial pride.
> Onward methinks, and diligently slow
> The firm connected bulwark seems to grow;
> Spreads its long arms amidst the watry roar,
> 290 Scoops out an empire, and usurps the shore.
> While the pent ocean rising o'er the pile,
> Sees an amphibious world beneath him smile;
> The slow canal, the yellow blossom'd vale,
> The willow tufted bank, the gliding sail,
> 295 The crowded mart, the cultivated plain,
> A new creation rescu'd from his reign.
>
> Thus, while around, the wave-subjected soil
> Impels the native to repeated toil,
> Industrious habits in each bosom reign,
> 300 And industry begets a love of gain.
> Hence all the good from opulence that springs,
> With all those ills superfluous treasure brings,
> Are here display'd. Their much-lov'd wealth imparts
> Convenience, plenty, elegance, and arts;
> 305 But view them closer, craft and fraud appear,
> Even liberty itself is barter'd here.
> At gold's superior charms all freedom flies,

286 *rampire:* rampart—the Dutch dykes.   *artificial:* not natural, produced by art.

290 *usurps:* takes the place of; i.e. creates a new shore-line.

297 *wave-subjected:* (1) subject to flooding; and (2) lying below sea-level (playing on Latin *subjectus*, and referring back to ll. 291-2).

305 ff. In 1758 Goldsmith had written of Holland: "No longer do we see there the industrious citizen planning schemes to defend his own liberty and the liberty of Europe, but the servile money-meditating miser, who desires riches to dissipate in luxury, and whose luxuries make him needy."

The needy sell it, and the rich man buys:
A land of tyrants, and a den of slaves,
310　Here wretches seek dishonourable graves,
And calmly bent, to servitude conform,
Dull as their lakes that slumber in the storm.

　　　Heavens! how unlike their Belgic sires of old!
Rough, poor, content, ungovernably bold;
315　War in each breast, and freedom on each brow;
How much unlike the sons of Britain now!

　　　Fir'd at the sound, my genius spreads her wing,
And flies where Britain courts the western spring;
Where lawns extend that scorn Arcadian pride,
320　And brighter streams than fam'd Hydaspis glide.
There all around the gentlest breezes stray,
There gentle music melts on every spray;
Creation's mildest charms are there combin'd,
Extremes are only in the master's mind!
325　Stern o'er each bosom reason holds her state.
With daring aims irregularly great,
Pride in their port, defiance in their eye,
I see the lords of human kind pass by,
Intent on high designs, a thoughtful band,
330　By forms unfashion'd, fresh from Nature's hand;

313 Belgic: Cæsar described the Belgæ as the bravest of the Gauls.

319 lawns: open grasslands, meadows.　　*Arcadia:* a province in ancient Greece, renowned for its beautiful countryside.

320 fam'd Hydaspis: (Hydaspes) the river Jhelum, in Pakistan. It was on the fringe of the known world for the Greeks and Romans (Alexander the Great turned back there from his conquests); hence Horace called it *fabulosus*.

324 The *master* is Man, the lord of creation.

327 port: carriage, bearing.

330 By forms unfashion'd: their behaviour and attitudes not moulded by conventions and formalities.

    Fierce in their native hardiness of soul,
    True to imagin'd right above controul,
    While even the peasant boasts these rights to scan,
    And learns to venerate himself as man.

335   Thine, Freedom, thine the blessings pictur'd here,
    Thine are those charms that dazzle and endear;
    Too blest indeed, were such without alloy,
    But foster'd even by Freedom ills annoy:
    That independence Britons prize too high,
340 Keeps man from man, and breaks the social tie;
    The self dependent lordlings stand alone,
    All claims that bind and sweeten life unknown;
    Here by the bonds of nature feebly held,
    Minds combat minds, repelling and repell'd;
345 Ferments arise, imprison'd factions roar,
    Represt ambition struggles round her shore,
    Till over-wrought, the general system feels
    Its motions stopt, or phrenzy fire the wheels.

    Nor this the worst. As nature's ties decay,
350 As duty, love, and honour fail to sway,
    Fictitious bonds, the bonds of wealth and law,
    Still gather strength, and force unwilling awe.
    Hence all obedience bows to these alone,
    And talent sinks, and merit weeps unknown;
355 Till Time may come, when, stript of all her charms,
    The land of scholars, and the nurse of arms;
    Where noble stems transmit the patriot flame,
    Where kings have toil'd, and poets wrote for fame;

  333 *scan:* perhaps here in the sense of "perceive, discern" (i.e. see and follow), rather than the more usual "scrutinize, test the value of".

  357 *Where noble stems transmit the patriot flame:* where patriotic ardour is inherited in noble families. These patriotic noblemen contrast with the *contending chiefs* of ll. 381 ff.

  358 *wrote*, where we would have *written*, was quite acceptable in eighteenth-century usage.

    One sink of level avarice shall lie,
360 And scholars, soldiers, kings unhonor'd die.

    Yet think not thus, when Freedom's ills I state,
I mean to flatter kings, or court the great;
Ye powers of truth that bid my soul aspire,
Far from my bosom drive the low desire;
365 And thou fair Freedom, taught alike to feel
The rabble's rage, and tyrant's angry steel;
Thou transitory flower, alike undone
By proud contempt, or favour's fostering sun,
Still may thy blooms the changeful clime endure,
370 I only would repress them to secure:
For just experience tells in every soil,
That those who think must govern those that toil,
And all that freedom's highest aims can reach,
Is but to lay proportion'd loads on each.
375 Hence, should one order disproportion'd grow,
Its double weight must ruin all below.

    O then how blind to all that truth requires,
Who think it freedom when a part aspires!
Calm is my soul, nor apt to rise in arms,
380 Except when fast approaching danger warms:
But when contending chiefs blockade the throne,
Contracting regal power to stretch their own,
When I behold a factious band agree
To call it freedom, when themselves are free;
385 Each wanton judge new penal statutes draw,
Laws grind the poor, and rich men rule the law;

375 The building metaphor is sustained in the word *order*; each architectural order, or system, represents a social class.

378 *when a part aspires:* when one section of society becomes ambitious and self-seeking.

381 ff. See Appendix A for an account of the political argument contained in these lines.

　　　　The wealth of climes, where savage nations roam,
　　　　Pillag'd from slaves, to purchase slaves at home;
　　　　Fear, pity, justice, indignation start,
390　　Tear off reserve, and bare my swelling heart;
　　　　'Till half a patriot, half a coward grown,
　　　　I fly from petty tyrants to the throne.

　　　　　Yes, brother, curse with me that baleful hour,
　　　　When first ambition struck at regal power;
395　　And thus, polluting honour in its source,
　　　　Gave wealth to sway the mind with double force.
　　　　Have we not seen, round Britain's peopled shore,
　　　　Her useful sons exchang'd for useless ore?
　　　　Seen all her triumphs but destruction haste,
400　　Like flaring tapers brightening as they waste;
　　　　Seen opulence, her grandeur to maintain,
　　　　Lead stern depopulation in her train,
　　　　And over fields, where scatter'd hamlets rose,
　　　　In barren solitary pomp repose?
405　　Have we not seen, at pleasure's lordly call,
　　　　The smiling long-frequented village fall;
　　　　Beheld the duteous son, the sire decay'd,
　　　　The modest matron, and the blushing maid,
　　　　Forc'd from their homes, a melancholy train,
410　　To traverse climes beyond the western main;
　　　　Where wild Oswego spreads her swamps around,
　　　　And Niagara stuns with thund'ring sound?

　　　　　Even now, perhaps, as there some pilgrim strays
　　　　Through tangled forests, and through dangerous ways;
415　　Where beasts with man divided empire claim,
　　　　And the brown Indian marks with murderous aim;

　396 *Gave:* "permitted", or perhaps "prompted".
　399 *Seen all her triumphs but destruction haste:* seen all her triumphs merely hasten destruction.
　411 *Oswego:* river in U.S.A., flowing into Lake Ontario.
　412 *Niagara:* there is no warrant for the pronunciation Níagára which the metre demands.

There, while above the giddy tempest flies,
And all around distressful yells arise,
The pensive exile, bending with his woe,
420 To stop too fearful, and too faint to go,
Casts a long look where England's glories shine,
And bids his bosom sympathize with mine.

   Vain, very vain, my weary search to find
That bliss which only centers in the mind:
425 Why have I stray'd, from pleasure and repose,
To seek a good each government bestows?
In every government, though terrors reign,
Though tyrant kings, or tyrant laws restrain,
How small, of all that human hearts endure,
430 That part which laws or kings can cause or cure.
Still to ourselves in every place consign'd,
Our own felicity we make or find:
With secret course, which no loud storms annoy,
Glides the smooth current of domestic joy.
435 The lifted ax, the agonizing wheel,
Luke's iron crown, and Damien's bed of steel,
To men remote from power but rarely known,
Leave reason, faith and conscience all our own.

420 According to Boswell, this line was contributed by Dr. Johnson. Goldsmith had written: "And faintly fainter, fainter seems to go".

429 ff. Johnson supplied the concluding lines, except for the penultimate couplet. The sentiments are similar to those in his *Rasselas*.

435 *wheel:* Capital punishment in France was by breaking on the wheel. Cf. Johnson's *London*, l. 108.

436 *Luke:* the brothers George and Luke Dozsa led a rebellion of peasants in Hungary in 1514. George (not Luke) was proclaimed King, and when the revolt was crushed he was tortured with a red-hot iron crown.   *Damien:* Robert-François Damiens, a fanatic tortured and executed in 1757 for the attempted assassination of Louis XV of France.

Edwin and Angelina

IN 1765 Goldsmith's friend Thomas Percy published his *Reliques of Ancient English Poetry*, a ballad-collection dedicated to the Countess of Northumberland, who subsequently appointed Percy chaplain and tutor in her household. Goldsmith, who was in financial difficulties, looked out a ballad he had previously written, and had a few copies privately printed "for the Amusement" of the same noble Lady—without, unfortunately, any beneficial result. The poem was revised and incorporated in *The Vicar of Wakefield*, where it is recited (ch. 8) by Mr. Burchell: English poetry, he declares, "is nothing at present but a combination of luxuriant images, without plot or connexion; a string of epithets that improve the sound, without carrying on the sense"—faults from which this ballad, "whatever be its other defects", is free. Goldsmith thought highly enough of the poem to include it in his anthology of *Poems for Young Ladies ... A Collection of the Best Pieces in our Language* (1766), where it stands first in the section devoted to Moral Poems.

As Percy later observed (*Reliques*, 3rd ed., 1775) Goldsmith is "indebted to the beautiful old ballad, *Gentle Herdsman*", which he much admired, "and has finely improved".

The text below, based on the first edition of *The Vicar of Wakefield* (1766), includes the numerous revisions which Goldsmith made for the second edition later in the same year.

"Turn, gentle hermit of the dale,
    And guide my lonely way,
To where yon taper cheers the vale,
    With hospitable ray.

5 "For here forlorn and lost I tread,
    With fainting steps and slow;
Where wilds immeasurably spread,
    Seem lengthening as I go."

"Forbear, my son," the hermit cries,
10   "To tempt the dangerous gloom;

3 The *taper*, which is also the *faithless phantom* of l. 11, is a will-o'-the-wisp.

For yonder faithless phantom flies
  To lure thee to thy doom.

"Here to the houseless child of want,
  My door is open still;
And tho' my portion is but scant,
  I give it with good will.

"Then turn to-night, and freely share
  Whate'er my cell bestows;
My rushy couch, and frugal fare,
  My blessing and repose.

"No flocks that range the valley free,
  To slaughter I condemn:
Taught by that power that pities me,
  I learn to pity them.

"But from the mountain's grassy side,
  A guiltless feast I bring;
A scrip with herbs and fruits supply'd,
  And water from the spring.

"Then, pilgrim, turn, thy cares forego;
  All earth-born cares are wrong:
Man wants but little here below,
  Nor wants that little long."

Soft as the dew from heav'n descends,
  His gentle accents fell:
The modest stranger lowly bends,
  And follows to the cell.

Far in a wilderness obscure
  The lonely mansion lay;
A refuge to the neighbouring poor,
  And strangers led astray.

27 *scrip:* small bag or satchel.
31-2 Adapted from a line in Edward Young's *Night Thoughts:* "Man wants but little; nor that little, long." (IV, 118.)
38 *mansion:* simply "house", "residence", with no suggestion of grandeur.

No stores beneath its humble thatch
    Requir'd a master's care;
The wicket opening with a latch,
    Receiv'd the harmless pair.

45 And now when busy crowds retire
    To take their evening rest,
The hermit trimm'd his little fire,
    And cheer'd his pensive guest:

And spread his vegetable store,
50   And gayly prest, and smil'd;
And skill'd in legendary lore,
    The lingering hours beguil'd.

Around in sympathetic mirth
    Its tricks the kitten tries,
55 The cricket chirrups in the hearth;
    The crackling faggot flies.

But nothing could a charm impart
    To sooth the stranger's woe;
For grief was heavy at his heart,
60   And tears began to flow.

His rising cares the hermit spy'd,
    With answering care opprest:
"And whence, unhappy youth," he cry'd,
    "The sorrows of thy breast?

65 "From better habitations spurn'd,
    Reluctant dost thou rove;
Or grieve for friendship unreturn'd,
    Or unregarded love?

"Alas! the joys that fortune brings,
70   Are trifling, and decay;
And those who prize the paltry things,
    More trifling still than they.

43 *wicket:* small door.

"And what is friendship but a name,
　　A charm that lulls to sleep;
75　A shade that follows wealth or fame,
　　But leaves the wretch to weep?

"And love is still an emptier sound,
　　The modern fair one's jest:
On earth unseen, or only found
80　　To warm the turtle's nest.

"For shame fond youth thy sorrows hush,
　　And spurn the sex," he said:
But while he spoke a rising blush
　　His love-lorn guest betray'd.

85　Surpriz'd he sees new beauties rise,
　　Swift mantling to the view;
Like colours o'er the morning skies,
　　As bright, as transient too.

The bashful look, the rising breast,
90　　Alternate spread alarms:
The lovely stranger stands confest
　　A maid in all her charms.

And "Ah, forgive a stranger rude,
　　A wretch forlorn," she cry'd;
95　"Whose feet unhallowed thus intrude
　　Where heaven and you reside.

"But let a maid thy pity share,
　　Whom love has taught to stray;
Who seeks for rest, but finds despair
100　　Companion of her way.

　80 *turtle*: the turtle-dove, emblem of constancy in love.
　85-6 The beauties of her complexion are revealed as she blushes. *mantling*: (1) of blood, suffusing the cheeks; (2) spreading over a surface.
　93 The first and second editions punctuate as follows: "And, ah, forgive . . ."

"My father liv'd beside the Tyne,
　　A wealthy Lord was he;
And all his wealth was mark'd as mine,
　　He had but only me.

105 "To win me from his tender arms,
　　Unnumber'd suitors came;
Who prais'd me for imputed charms,
　　And felt or feign'd a flame.

"Each hour a mercenary crowd
110　With richest proffers strove:
Amongst the rest young Edwin bow'd,
　　But never talk'd of love.

"In humble simplest habit clad,
　　No wealth nor power had he;
115 Wisdom and worth were all he had,
　　But these were all to me.

"The blossom opening to the day,
　　The dews of heaven refin'd,
Could nought of purity display,
120　To emulate his mind.

"The dew, the blossom on the tree,
　　With charms inconstant shine;
Their charms were his, but woe to me,
　　Their constancy was mine.

116 The text printed in *The Miscellaneous Works of Goldsmith* (1801) includes at this point an additional stanza, written some years after the rest of the poem, and said to have been presented by Goldsmith to a friend:

　　　　And when, beside me in the dale,
　　　　　He carol'd lays of love,
　　　　His breath lent fragrance to the gale,
　　　　　And music to the grove.

125 "For still I try'd each fickle art,
          Importunate and vain;
    And while his passion touch'd my heart,
          I triumph'd in his pain.

    "Till quite dejected with my scorn,
130   He left me to my pride;
    And sought a solitude forlorn,
          In secret where he died.

    "But mine the sorrow, mine the fault,
          And well my life shall pay;
135 I'll seek the solitude he sought,
          And stretch me where he lay.

    "And there forlorn despairing hid,
          I'll lay me down and die:
    'Twas so for me that Edwin did,
140   And so for him will I."

    "Forbid it heaven!" the hermit cry'd,
          And clasp'd her to his breast:
    The wondering fair one turn'd to chide,
          'Twas Edwin's self that prest.

145 "Turn, Angelina, ever dear,
          My charmer, turn to see,
    Thy own, thy long-lost Edwin here,
          Restor'd to love and thee.

    "Thus let me hold thee to my heart,
150   And ev'ry care resign:
    And shall we never, never part,
          My life,—my all that's mine.

    "No, never, from this hour to part,
          We'll live and love so true;
155 The sigh that rends thy constant heart,
          Shall break thy Edwin's too."

An Elegy on the Death of a Mad Dog

GOLDSMITH ridiculed the hysterical fear of mad dogs in 1760, when there was a widespread scare (see *The Citizen of the World*, Letter 69); he may have written this poem at about the same time. It first appeared in *The Vicar of Wakefield*, where it is recited in ch. 17 by the Vicar's youngest son, with the approval of his father: "A very good boy, Bill, upon my word, and an elegy that may truly be called tragical". The text incorporates the felicitous alteration of l. 19 which Goldsmith made for the second edition of *The Vicar* (1766).

> Good people all, of every sort,
>   Give ear unto my song;
> And if you find it wond'rous short,
>   It cannot hold you long.
>
> 5 In Isling town there was a man,
>   Of whom the world might say,
> That still a godly race he ran,
>   Whene'er he went to pray.
>
> A kind and gentle heart he had,
> 10 To comfort friends and foes;
> The naked every day he clad,
>   When he put on his cloaths.
>
> And in that town a dog was found,
>   As many dogs there be,
> 15 Both mungrel, puppy, whelp, and hound,
>   And curs of low degree.

5 Goldsmith had lodgings in Islington from 1763-4; it was then a country village on the northern fringe of London.

> This dog and man at first were friends;
>   But when a pique began,
> The dog, to gain some private ends,
> 20   Went mad and bit the man.
>
> Around from all the neighbouring streets,
>   The wondering neighbours ran,
> And swore the dog had lost his wits,
>   To bite so good a man.
>
> 25 The wound it seem'd both sore and sad,
>   To every christian eye;
> And while they swore the dog was mad,
>   They swore the man would die.
>
> But soon a wonder came to light,
> 30   That shew'd the rogues they lied,
> The man recovered of the bite,
>   The dog it was that dy'd.

18 *pique:* quarrel.
19 The first edition reads: "The dog, to gain his private ends".

Song

FROM *The Vicar of Wakefield* (1766), vol. II, ch. 5. It is sung, after her return home, by the Vicar's daughter Olivia, who has herself stooped to folly.

> When lovely woman stoops to folly,
>   And finds too late that men betray,
> What charm can sooth her melancholy,
>   What art can wash her guilt away?
>
> 5 The only art her guilt to cover,
>   To hide her shame from every eye,
> To give repentance to her lover,
>   And wring his bosom—is to die.

Epilogue to The Good Natur'd Man

GOLDSMITH's comedy *The Good Natur'd Man* was first performed at Covent Garden Theatre on January 29, 1768. It was published on February 5, though the Epilogue and Johnson's Prologue had already appeared, in slightly garbled versions, in two newspapers of February 3. Goldsmith added a note explaining that "The Author, in expectation of an Epilogue from a Friend at Oxford, deferred writing one himself till the very last hour. What is here offered, owes all its success to the graceful manner of the Actress who spoke it."

The text follows the first edition, except for the final line which read originally: "And view with favour, the Good-natur'd Man"; it was revised for the fifth edition, later in 1768.

>   As puffing quacks some caitiff wretch procure
>   To swear the pill, or drop, has wrought a cure;
>   Thus on the stage, our play-wrights still depend
>   For Epilogues and Prologues on some friend,
> 5   Who knows each art of coaxing up the town,
>   And make full many a bitter pill go down.
>   Conscious of this, our bard has gone about,
>   And teaz'd each rhyming friend to help him out.
>   An Epilogue, things can't go on without it;
> 10 It cou'd not fail, wou'd you but set about it.
>   Young man, cries one (a bard laid up in clover)
>   Alas, young man, my writing days are over;
>   Let boys play tricks, and kick the straw, not I;
>   Your brother Doctor there, perhaps, may try.
> 15 What I! dear Sir, the Doctor interposes,
>   What, plant my thistle, Sir, among his roses!

1 i.e. as quack-doctors, advertising their wares with false claims, get hold of (and bribe) some poor wretch. . . .

2 *drop:* medicine, to be taken in drops.

9 At this point the Epilogue slips into direct speech as the poet canvasses his friends.

13 *kick the straw:* show their mettle, like young colts—and unlike an old horse "laid up in clover".

No, no, I've other contests to maintain;
To-night I head our troops at Warwick-Lane.
Go, ask your manager—Who, me? your pardon;
20 Those things are not our fort at Covent-Garden.
Our Author's friends, thus plac'd at happy distance,
Give him good words indeed, but no assistance.
As some unhappy wight, at some new play,
At the Pit door stands elbowing away,
25 While oft, with many a smile, and many a shrug,
He eyes the centre, where his friends sit snug,
His simpering friends, with pleasure in their eyes,
Sink as he sinks, and as he rises rise:
He nods, they nod; he cringes, they grimace;
30 But not a soul will budge to give him place.
Since then, unhelp'd, our bard must now conform
To 'bide the pelting of this pittiless storm,
Blame where you must, be candid where you can,
And be each critick the Good-natur'd Man.

18 *Warwick-Lane:* at this time the site of the Royal College of Physicians, London. There was a long-standing dispute between the Fellows and the Licentiates of the College. The "thistle" of l. 16 seems to refer to some Scotch physician who was a friend of the poet's, but there is no obvious candidate.

19 *manager:* George Colman, the manager of the Covent Garden Theatre. **20** *fort:* forte.

23 *wight:* man—an archaism, often used (as here) to suggest pity or contempt.

28 i.e. his sympathetic friends share his moods of dejection and new hope. Goldsmith seems to be echoing the Earl of Roscommon's *Essay on Translated Verse* (1684), l. 225: "Fall, when he falls; and when he rises, rise."

29 *cringes:* bows deferentially.

32 Quoted from *King Lear*, III, iv.

33 An adaptation of Pope's line "Laugh where we must, be candid where we can" (*Essay on Man*, Epistle I, l. 15).   *candid:* favourably disposed, kindly.

Epilogue to The Sister

The Sister, a sentimental (and insipid) comedy by Mrs. Charlotte Lennox, was performed on February 18, 1769, and withdrawn after one night; it was published later the same year. The plot of the comedy hinges on assumed names—which may have suggested the theme of the Epilogue.

    What! five long acts—and all to make us wiser!
    Our authoress sure has wanted an adviser.
    Had she consulted *me*, she should have made
    Her moral play a speaking masquerade;
5 Warm'd up each bustling scene, and in her rage
    Have emptied all the Green-room on the stage.
    My life on't, this had kept her play from sinking,
    Have pleas'd our eyes, and sav'd the pain of thinking.
    Well, since she thus has shewn her want of skill,
10 What if I give a masquerade? I will.
    But how! ay, there's the rub! (*pausing*) I've got my cue:
    The world's a masquerade! the masquers, you, you, you.
                        [*To Boxes, Pit, Gall.*
    Lud! what a groupe the motley scene discloses!
    False wits, false wives, false virgins, and false spouses:
15 Statesmen with bridles on; and, close beside 'em,
    Patriots, in party colour'd suits, that ride 'em.
    There Hebes, turn'd of fifty, try once more,
    To raise a flame in Cupids of threescore.

  6 *Green-room:* room in theatre for actors when off stage; here = the whole acting company, with its stock of costumes, etc.

  16 *Patriots:* various political groups in the eighteenth century assumed this title (especially if they claimed to defend individual liberty), but as they did not always live up to their principles the term came into disrepute: "it is sometimes used for a factious disturber of the government" (Johnson's *Dictionary*). *party colour'd:* variegated—with a pun on political "party", and an allusion to the motley traditionally worn by Fools.

  17 *Hebe* was the goddess of youth. The principal comic character in *The Sister*, Lady Autumn, is "a coquet of fifty".

These, in their turn, with appetites as keen,
20 Deserting fifty, fasten on fifteen.
Miss, not yet full fifteen, with fire uncommon,
Flings down her sampler, and takes up the woman:
The little urchin smiles, and spreads her lure,
And tries to kill ere she's got power to cure.
25 Thus 'tis with all—Their chief and constant care
Is to seem every thing—but what they are.
Yon broad, bold, angry spark, I fix my eye on,
Who seems t' have robb'd his vizor from the lion,
Who frowns, and talks, and swears, with round parade,
30 Looking, as who should say, *Damme! who's afraid!*
                                    [*mimicking.*
Strip but his vizor off, and sure I am,
You'll find his lionship a very lamb.
Yon politician, famous in debate,
Perhaps to vulgar eyes bestrides the state;
35 Yet, when he deigns his real shape t' assume,
He turns old woman, and bestrides a broom.
Yon patriot too, who presses on your sight,
And seems to every gazer all in white;
If with a bribe his candour you attack,
40 He bows, turns round, and whip—the man's a black!
Yon critic too—but whither do I run?
If I proceed, our bard will be undone!
Well then, a truce, since she requests it too;
Do you spare her, and I'll for once spare you.

27 *spark:* "A lively, showy, splendid, gay man. It is commonly used in contempt" (Johnson's *Dictionary*).
28 *vizor:* mask.
39 *candour:* integrity, impartiality—with a play on the word's etymology (Latin *candor*, dazzling whiteness).

The Deserted Village

PUBLISHED on May 26, 1770, *The Deserted Village* was an immediate success; by the end of the year it had gone through nine authorised editions. The revisions which Goldsmith made for the second and fourth editions are incorporated in the text below.

As early as 1762 Goldsmith had deplored the dispossession of villagers by wealthy landlords who wanted to enlarge and beautify their estates (see "The Revolution in Low Life", in R. S. Crane's edition of *New Essays by Oliver Goldsmith*, Chicago, 1927); and he had returned to the theme of depopulation at the close of *The Traveller* (1764).

TO
SIR JOSHUA REYNOLDS

DEAR SIR,

I can have no expectations in an address of this kind, either to add to your reputation, or to establish my own. You can gain nothing from my admiration, as I am ignorant of that art in which you are said to excel; and I may lose much by the
5 severity of your judgment, as few have a juster taste in poetry than you. Setting interest therefore aside, to which I never paid much attention, I must be indulged at present in following my affections. The only dedication I ever made was to my brother, because I loved him better than most other men. He is since
10 dead. Permit me to inscribe this Poem to you.

How far you may be pleased with the versification and mere mechanical parts of this attempt, I don't pretend to enquire; but I know you will object (and indeed several of our best and wisest friends concur in the opinion) that the depopulation it
15 deplores is no where to be seen, and the disorders it laments are

REYNOLDS: Sir Joshua Reynolds (1723-92), the famous painter, and an intimate friend of Goldsmith.

6 *interest:* self-interest.

9-10 The Reverend Henry Goldsmith, to whom *The Traveller* was dedicated, died in May 1768.

only to be found in the poet's own imagination. To this I can scarce make any other answer than that I sincerely believe what I have written; that I have taken all possible pains, in my country excursions, for these four or five years past, to be certain of what I alledge, and that all my views and enquiries have led me to believe those miseries real, which I here attempt to display. But this is not the place to enter into an enquiry, whether the country be depopulating, or not; the discussion would take up much room, and I should prove myself, at best, an indifferent politician, to tire the reader with a long preface, when I want his unfatigued attention to a long poem.

In regretting the depopulation of the country, I inveigh against the increase of our luxuries; and here also I expect the shout of modern politicians against me. For twenty or thirty years past, it has been the fashion to consider luxury as one of the greatest national advantages; and all the wisdom of antiquity in that particular, as erroneous. Still however, I must remain a professed ancient on that head, and continue to think those luxuries prejudicial to states, by which so many vices are introduced, and so many kingdoms have been undone. Indeed so much has been poured out of late on the other side of the question, that, merely for the sake of novelty and variety, one would sometimes wish to be in the right.

I am,

Dear Sir,

Your sincere friend,

and ardent admirer,

OLIVER GOLDSMITH.

The Deserted Village

Sweet AUBURN, loveliest village of the plain,
Where health and plenty cheared the labouring swain,
Where smiling spring its earliest visit paid,
And parting summer's lingering blooms delayed,
5 Dear lovely bowers of innocence and ease,
Seats of my youth, when every sport could please,
How often have I loitered o'er thy green,
Where humble happiness endeared each scene;
How often have I paused on every charm,
10 The sheltered cot, the cultivated farm,
The never failing brook, the busy mill,
The decent church that topt the neighbouring hill,
The hawthorn bush, with seats beneath the shade,
For talking age and whispering lovers made.
15 How often have I blest the coming day,
When toil remitting lent its turn to play,
And all the village train from labour free
Led up their sports beneath the spreading tree,
While many a pastime circled in the shade,
20 The young contending as the old surveyed;
And many a gambol frolicked o'er the ground,
And slights of art and feats of strength went round.

1 AUBURN: Goldsmith was certainly thinking of Lissoy, the Irish village where he was brought up, many of whose inhabitants were dispossessed by the local landowner. But since the poet claimed to have seen deserted villages in England, we may consider Auburn as at once a particular and a typical village.

10 *cot:* cottage.

12 *decent:* (1) pleasant in appearance; (2) modest, in keeping with its surroundings.

18 *Led up:* led off, began.

22 *slights:* sleights.

And still as each repeated pleasure tired,
Succeeding sports the mirthful band inspired;
25 The dancing pair that simply sought renown
By holding out to tire each other down,
The swain mistrustless of his smutted face,
While secret laughter tittered round the place,
The bashful virgin's side-long looks of love,
30 The matron's glance that would those looks reprove.
These were thy charms, sweet village; sports like these,
With sweet succession, taught even toil to please;
These round thy bowers their chearful influence shed,
These were thy charms—But all these charms are fled.

35 Sweet smiling village, loveliest of the lawn,
Thy sports are fled, and all thy charms withdrawn;
Amidst thy bowers the tyrant's hand is seen,
And desolation saddens all thy green:
One only master grasps the whole domain,
40 And half a tillage stints thy smiling plain;
No more thy glassy brook reflects the day,
But choaked with sedges, works its weedy way.
Along thy glades, a solitary guest,
The hollow sounding bittern guards its nest;
45 Amidst thy desert walks the lapwing flies,
And tires their ecchoes with unvaried cries.
Sunk are thy bowers in shapeless ruin all,
And the long grass o'ertops the mouldering wall,
And trembling, shrinking from the spoiler's hand,
50 Far, far away thy children leave the land.

25 *simply:* in a simple, unsophisticated way.
27-8 A practical joke, in which the victim is tricked into smearing his face with soot.   *mistrustless:* unsuspecting.
35 *lawn:* plain; open grassland.
40 Only half the land is now under cultivation, and the prosperity of the area is therefore greatly reduced.
43-6 See Appendix B for Goldsmith's prose descriptions of the bittern and lapwing.

>
> Ill fares the land, to hastening ills a prey,
> Where wealth accumulates, and men decay;
> Princes and lords may flourish, or may fade;
> A breath can make them, as a breath has made.
> 55 But a bold peasantry, their country's pride,
> When once destroyed, can never be supplied.
>
> A time there was, ere England's griefs began,
> When every rood of ground maintained its man;
> For him light labour spread her wholesome store,
> 60 Just gave what life required, but gave no more:
> His best companions, innocence and health;
> And his best riches, ignorance of wealth.
>
> But times are altered; trade's unfeeling train
> Usurp the land and dispossess the swain;
> 65 Along the lawn, where scattered hamlets rose,
> Unwieldy wealth, and cumbrous pomp repose;
> And every want to oppulence allied,
> And every pang that folly pays to pride.
> Those gentle hours that plenty bade to bloom,
> 70 Those calm desires that asked but little room,
> Those healthful sports that graced the peaceful scene,
> Lived in each look, and brightened all the green;
> These far departing seek a kinder shore,
> And rural mirth and manners are no more.
>
> 75 Sweet AUBURN! parent of the blissful hour,
> Thy glades forlorn confess the tyrant's power.
> Here as I take my solitary rounds,
> Amidst thy tangling walks, and ruined grounds,

66 *cumbrous:* cumbersome, oppressive.

69 *Those:* All the authoritative editions read "These", which would seem to be a misprint.

74 *manners:* (1) habits, customs; (2) codes of behaviour and morality—i.e. the whole rural way of life.

And, many a year elapsed, return to view
80 Where once the cottage stood, the hawthorn grew,
Remembrance wakes with all her busy train,
Swells at my breast, and turns the past to pain.

In all my wanderings round this world of care,
In all my griefs—and GOD has given my share—
85 I still had hopes my latest hours to crown,
Amidst these humble bowers to lay me down;
To husband out life's taper at the close,
And keep the flame from wasting by repose.
I still had hopes, for pride attends us still,
90 Amidst the swains to shew my book-learned skill,
Around my fire an evening groupe to draw,
And tell of all I felt, and all I saw;
And, as an hare whom hounds and horns pursue,
Pants to the place from whence at first she flew,
95 I still had hopes, my long vexations past,
Here to return—and die at home at last.

O blest retirement, friend to life's decline,
Retreats from care that never must be mine,
How happy he who crowns in shades likes these,
100 A youth of labour with an age of ease;
Who quits a world where strong temptations try,
And, since 'tis hard to combat, learns to fly.
For him no wretches, born to work and weep,
Explore the mine, or tempt the dangerous deep;
105 No surly porter stands in guilty state
To spurn imploring famine from the gate;
But on he moves to meet his latter end,
Angels around befriending virtue's friend;
Bends to the grave with unperceived decay,
110 While resignation gently slopes the way;

104 *tempt:* (1) attempt, venture on; (2) provoke (by their presence).
109 Cf. Johnson, *Vanity of Human Wishes*, l. 293: "An age that melts with unperceiv'd decay".

    And all his prospects brightening to the last,
    His Heaven commences ere the world be past!

    Sweet was the sound when oft at evening's close,
    Up yonder hill the village murmur rose;
115 There as I past with careless steps and slow,
    The mingling notes came softened from below;
    The swain responsive as the milk-maid sung,
    The sober herd that lowed to meet their young;
    The noisy geese that gabbled o'er the pool,
120 The playful children just let loose from school;
    The watch-dog's voice that bayed the whispering wind,
    And the loud laugh that spoke the vacant mind,
    These all in sweet confusion sought the shade,
    And filled each pause the nightingale had made.
125 But now the sounds of population fail,
    No chearful murmurs fluctuate in the gale,
    No busy steps the grass-grown foot-way tread,
    For all the bloomy flush of life is fled.
    All but yon widowed, solitary thing
130 That feebly bends beside the plashy spring;
    She, wretched matron, forced, in age, for bread,
    To strip the brook with mantling cresses spread,
    To pick her wintry faggot from the thorn,
    To seek her nightly shed, and weep till morn;
135 She only left of all the harmless train,
    The sad historian of the pensive plain.

    Near yonder copse, where once the garden smil'd,
    And still where many a garden flower grows wild;
    There, where a few torn shrubs the place disclose,

---

115 *careless:* carefree.
117 *responsive:* singing in response.
122 *vacant* (and 257): carefree.
123 *confusion:* a blending or mingling together.
126 *gale* (and 400): simply "wind": see *The Traveller*, l. 47, note.
130 *plashy:* marshy.
132 *mantling cresses:* watercress covering the surface of the brook.

140 The village preacher's modest mansion rose.
　　 A man he was, to all the country dear,
　　 And passing rich with forty pounds a year;
　　 Remote from towns he ran his godly race,
　　 Nor e'er had changed, nor wish'd to change his place;
145 Unpractised he to fawn, or seek for power,
　　 By doctrines fashioned to the varying hour;
　　 Far other aims his heart had learned to prize,
　　 More skilled to raise the wretched than to rise.
　　 His house was known to all the vagrant train,
150 He chid their wanderings, but relieved their pain;
　　 The long remembered beggar was his guest,
　　 Whose beard descending swept his aged breast;
　　 The ruined spendthrift, now no longer proud,
　　 Claimed kindred there, and had his claims allowed;
155 The broken soldier, kindly bade to stay,
　　 Sate by his fire, and talked the night away;
　　 Wept o'er his wounds, or tales of sorrow done,
　　 Shouldered his crutch, and shewed how fields were won.
　　 Pleased with his guests, the good man learned to glow,
160 And quite forgot their vices in their woe;
　　 Careless their merits, or their faults to scan,
　　 His pity gave ere charity began.

　　　　Thus to relieve the wretched was his pride,
　　 And even his failings leaned to Virtue's side;
165 But in his duty prompt at every call,
　　 He watched and wept, he prayed and felt, for all.

140 *mansion:* (also ll. 195, 238) house, dwelling.

142 *passing:* exceedingly, surpassingly.

155 The disbanded ("broken") soldier turned beggar was a familiar sight in the countryside.

161 *Careless:* not concerning himself.

162 He relieves the wants of his guests with generous impulsiveness, out of pity for their woes; the strictly charitable man would pause to consider the merits of their cases. On Goldsmith's preoccupation with benevolence and prudence see McD. Emslie, *Goldsmith: The Vicar of Wakefield* (London, 1963), pp. 52 ff.

And, as a bird each fond endearment tries,
To tempt its new fledged offspring to the skies;
He tried each art, reproved each dull delay,
170 Allured to brighter worlds, and led the way.

Beside the bed where parting life was layed,
And sorrow, guilt, and pain, by turns dismayed,
The reverend champion stood. At his control,
Despair and anguish fled the struggling soul;
175 Comfort came down the trembling wretch to raise,
And his last faultering accents whispered praise.

At church, with meek and unaffected grace,
His looks adorned the venerable place;
Truth from his lips prevailed with double sway,
180 And fools, who came to scoff, remained to pray.
The service past, around the pious man,
With steady zeal each honest rustic ran;
Even children followed with endearing wile,
And plucked his gown, to share the good man's smile.
185 His ready smile a parent's warmth exprest,
Their welfare pleased him, and their cares distrest;
To them his heart, his love, his griefs were given,
But all his serious thoughts had rest in Heaven.
As some tall cliff that lifts its awful form,
190 Swells from the vale, and midway leaves the storm,
Tho' round its breast the rolling clouds are spread,
Eternal sunshine settles on its head.

Beside yon straggling fence that skirts the way,
With blossomed furze unprofitably gay,
195 There, in his noisy mansion, skill'd to rule,
The village master taught his little school;
A man severe he was, and stern to view,
I knew him well, and every truant knew;
Well had the boding tremblers learned to trace

179 *with double sway:* because he practised what he preached.
199 *boding:* anticipating trouble.

200 The day's disasters in his morning face;
Full well they laugh'd with counterfeited glee,
At all his jokes, for many a joke had he;
Full well the busy whisper circling round,
Conveyed the dismal tidings when he frowned;
205 Yet he was kind, or if severe in aught,
The love he bore to learning was in fault;
The village all declared how much he knew;
'Twas certain he could write, and cypher too;
Lands he could measure, terms and tides presage,
210 And even the story ran that he could gauge.
In arguing too, the parson owned his skill,
For e'en tho' vanquished, he could argue still;
While words of learned length, and thundering sound,
Amazed the gazing rustics ranged around,
215 And still they gazed, and still the wonder grew,
That one small head could carry all he knew.

But past is all his fame. The very spot
Where many a time he triumphed, is forgot.
Near yonder thorn, that lifts its head on high,
220 Where once the sign-post caught the passing eye,
Low lies that house where nut-brown draughts inspired,
Where grey-beard mirth and smiling toil retired,
Where village statesmen talked with looks profound,
And news much older than their ale went round.
225 Imagination fondly stoops to trace
The parlour splendours of that festive place;
The white-washed wall, the nicely sanded floor,
The varnished clock that clicked behind the door;
The chest contrived a double debt to pay,
230 A bed by night, a chest of drawers by day;

208 *cypher:* do calculations.
209 *terms:* days fixed for the payment of rent, etc.   *tides:* probably Church festivals (e.g. Whitsuntide).
210 *gauge:* measure; more specifically, measure the contents of a barrel, cask, etc.

The pictures placed for ornament and use,
The twelve good rules, the royal game of goose;
The hearth, except when winter chill'd the day,
With aspen boughs, and flowers, and fennel gay,
235 While broken tea-cups, wisely kept for shew,
Ranged o'er the chimney, glistened in a row.

Vain transitory splendours! Could not all
Reprieve the tottering mansion from its fall!
Obscure it sinks, nor shall it more impart
240 An hour's importance to the poor man's heart;
Thither no more the peasant shall repair
To sweet oblivion of his daily care;
No more the farmer's news, the barber's tale,
No more the wood-man's ballad shall prevail;
245 No more the smith his dusky brow shall clear,
Relax his ponderous strength, and lean to hear;
The host himself no longer shall be found
Careful to see the mantling bliss go round;
Nor the coy maid, half willing to be prest,
250 Shall kiss the cup to pass it to the rest.

Yes! let the rich deride, the proud disdain,
These simple blessings of the lowly train,
To me more dear, congenial to my heart,
One native charm, than all the gloss of art;
255 Spontaneous joys, where Nature has its play,
The soul adopts, and owns their first born sway,
Lightly they frolic o'er the vacant mind,
Unenvied, unmolested, unconfined.
But the long pomp, the midnight masquerade,
260 With all the freaks of wanton wealth arrayed,

232 See p. 82, "A Description of an Author's Bedchamber", ll. 11-12 and notes.

234 *fennel:* a fragrant and decorative plant with yellow flowers.
248 *mantling:* foaming.
260 *wanton:* (1) luxurious; (2) self-indulgent, capricious; (3) lascivious.

In these, ere triflers half their wish obtain,
The toiling pleasure sickens into pain;
And, even while fashion's brightest arts decoy,
The heart distrusting asks, if this be joy.

265   Ye friends to truth, ye statesmen who survey
The rich man's joys encrease, the poor's decay,
'Tis yours to judge, how wide the limits stand
Between a splendid and an happy land.
Proud swells the tide with loads of freighted ore,
270 And shouting Folly hails them from her shore;
Hoards, even beyond the miser's wish abound,
And rich men flock from all the world around.
Yet count our gains. This wealth is but a name
That leaves our useful products still the same.
275 Not so the loss. The man of wealth and pride,
Takes up a space that many poor supplied;
Space for his lake, his park's extended bounds,
Space for his horses, equipage, and hounds;
The robe that wraps his limbs in silken sloth,
280 Has robbed the neighbouring fields of half their growth;
His seat, where solitary sports are seen,
Indignant spurns the cottage from the green;
Around the world each needful product flies,
For all the luxuries the world supplies.
285 While thus the land adorned for pleasure all
In barren splendour feebly waits the fall.

As some fair female unadorned and plain,
Secure to please while youth confirms her reign,
Slights every borrowed charm that dress supplies,
290 Nor shares with art the triumph of her eyes.
But when those charms are past, for charms are frail,
When time advances, and when lovers fail,

278 *equipage:* coach.
281 *seat:* country house.
288 *Secure:* confident, sure.

>   She then shines forth sollicitous to bless,
>   In all the glaring impotence of dress.
> 295 Thus fares the land, by luxury betrayed,
>   In nature's simplest charms at first arrayed,
>   But verging to decline, its splendours rise,
>   Its vistas strike, its palaces surprize;
>   While scourged by famine from the smiling land,
> 300 The mournful peasant leads his humble band;
>   And while he sinks without one arm to save,
>   The country blooms—a garden, and a grave.
>
>   Where then, ah, where shall poverty reside,
>   To scape the pressure of contiguous pride?
> 305 If to some common's fenceless limits strayed,
>   He drives his flock to pick the scanty blade,
>   Those fenceless fields the sons of wealth divide,
>   And even the bare-worn common is denied.
>
>   If to the city sped—What waits him there?
> 310 To see profusion that he must not share;
>   To see ten thousand baneful arts combined
>   To pamper luxury, and thin mankind;
>   To see those joys the sons of pleasure know,
>   Extorted from his fellow-creature's woe.
> 315 Here, while the courtier glitters in brocade,
>   There the pale artist plies the sickly trade;

293 *sollicitous to bless:* anxious to please.

298 *vistas:* views (especially through woods, or along avenues of trees) created for picturesque effect by landscape-gardeners.

304 *contiguous:* neighbouring, adjacent.

305 ff. Under the open-field system of agriculture many cottagers grazed animals on the village common. They lost this privilege (often without compensation) when commons and waste ground were enclosed by large landowners. Enclosing was particularly vigorous in the period 1765-74.

311 *baneful:* destructive, ruinous.

316 The health of the craftsman who supplies the luxury goods is ruined by his work.

Here, while the proud their long drawn pomps display,
There the black gibbet glooms beside the way.
The dome where pleasure holds her midnight reign,
320 Here richly deckt admits the gorgeous train,
Tumultuous grandeur crowds the blazing square,
The rattling chariots clash, the torches glare;
Sure scenes like these no troubles e'er annoy!
Sure these denote one universal joy!
325 Are these thy serious thoughts?—Ah, turn thine eyes
Where the poor houseless shivering female lies.
She once, perhaps, in village plenty blest,
Has wept at tales of innocence distrest;
Her modest looks the cottage might adorn,
330 Sweet as the primrose peeps beneath the thorn;
Now lost to all; her friends, her virtue fled,
Near her betrayer's door she lays her head,
And pinch'd with cold, and shrinking from the shower,
With heavy heart deplores that luckless hour,
335 When idly first, ambitious of the town,
She left her wheel and robes of country brown.

Do thine, sweet AUBURN, thine, the loveliest train,
Do thy fair tribes participate her pain?
Even now, perhaps, by cold and hunger led,
340 At proud men's doors they ask a little bread!

318 As a deterrent to crime the bodies of murderers and notorious thieves were hung in chains on gibbets, usually in some prominent place, and sometimes for as long as a whole year. The force of the juxtaposition of wealthy display and the black gibbet is brought out by the crime statistics for London and Middlesex: "Out of 678 capital sentences from 1749-1771, 584 were for offences against property" (L. Radzinowicz, *A History of English Criminal Law*, London, 1948-56, vol. I, p. 148. See also pp. 215-19).

319 *dome:* mansion—though Goldsmith may have been thinking of the famous Rotunda in Ranelagh Gardens, used for masquerades and balls during the second half of the eighteenth century.

322 *chariots:* coaches.

336 *wheel:* spinning-wheel.

        Ah, no. To distant climes, a dreary scene,
Where half the convex world intrudes between,
Through torrid tracts with fainting steps they go,
Where wild Altama murmurs to their woe.
345 Far different there from all that charm'd before,
The various terrors of that horrid shore;
Those blazing suns that dart a downward ray,
And fiercely shed intolerable day;
Those matted woods where birds forget to sing,
350 But silent bats in drowsy clusters cling,
Those poisonous fields with rank luxuriance crowned,
Where the dark scorpion gathers death around;
Where at each step the stranger fears to wake
The rattling terrors of the vengeful snake;
355 Where crouching tigers wait their hapless prey,
And savage men more murderous still than they;
While oft in whirls the mad tornado flies,
Mingling the ravaged landscape with the skies.
Far different these from every former scene,
360 The cooling brook, the grassy-vested green,
The breezy covert of the warbling grove,
That only sheltered thefts of harmless love.

        Good Heaven! what sorrows gloom'd that parting day,
That called them from their native walks away;
365 When the poor exiles, every pleasure past,
Hung round their bowers, and fondly looked their last,
And took a long farewell, and wished in vain
For seats like these beyond the western main;
And shuddering still to face the distant deep,
370 Returned and wept, and still returned to weep.

344 *Altama:* the Altamaha, a river in Georgia, U.S.A. General James Oglethorpe (later a friend of both Johnson and Goldsmith) founded the colony of Georgia in 1733.

355 *tigers:* cougars. In his *History of the Earth* Goldsmith says that this mammal "is usually called the Red Tiger.... Of all the American animals, this is the most formidable and mischievous."

> The good old sire the first prepared to go
> To new found worlds, and wept for others' woe.
> But for himself, in conscious virtue brave,
> He only wished for worlds beyond the grave.
> 375 His lovely daughter, lovelier in her tears,
> The fond companion of his helpless years,
> Silent went next, neglectful of her charms,
> And left a lover's for a father's arms.
> With louder plaints the mother spoke her woes,
> 380 And blest the cot where every pleasure rose;
> And kist her thoughtless babes with many a tear,
> And claspt them close in sorrow doubly dear;
> Whilst her fond husband strove to lend relief
> In all the silent manliness of grief.
>
> 385 O luxury! Thou curst by Heaven's decree,
> How ill exchanged are things like these for thee!
> How do thy potions with insidious joy,
> Diffuse their pleasures only to destroy!
> Kingdoms by thee, to sickly greatness grown,
> 390 Boast of a florid vigour not their own.
> At every draught more large and large they grow,
> A bloated mass of rank unwieldy woe;
> Till sapped their strength, and every part unsound,
> Down, down they sink, and spread a ruin round.
>
> 395 Even now the devastation is begun,
> And half the business of destruction done;
> Even now, methinks, as pondering here I stand,
> I see the rural virtues leave the land.
> Down where yon anchoring vessel spreads the sail,
> 400 That idly waiting flaps with every gale,
> Downward they move, a melancholy band,
> Pass from the shore, and darken all the strand.

402 The emigrant band moves down from the edge of dry land on to the beach. *Strand* in the sense of "beach" is still current in the south of Ireland.

        Contented toil, and hospitable care,
        And kind connubial tenderness, are there;
405 And piety with wishes placed above,
        And steady loyalty, and faithful love.
        And thou, sweet Poetry, thou loveliest maid,
        Still first to fly where sensual joys invade;
        Unfit in these degenerate times of shame,
410 To catch the heart, or strike for honest fame;
        Dear charming nymph, neglected and decried,
        My shame in crowds, my solitary pride;
        Thou source of all my bliss, and all my woe,
        That found'st me poor at first, and keep'st me so;
415 Thou guide by which the nobler arts excell,
        Thou nurse of every virtue, fare thee well.
        Farewell, and O where'er thy voice be tried,
        On Torno's cliffs, or Pambamarca's side,
        Whether where equinoctial fervours glow,
420 Or winter wraps the polar world in snow,
        Still let thy voice prevailing over time,
        Redress the rigours of the inclement clime;
        Aid slighted truth, with thy persuasive strain
        Teach erring man to spurn the rage of gain;
425 Teach him that states of native strength possest,
        Tho' very poor, may still be very blest;
        That trade's proud empire hastes to swift decay,
        As ocean sweeps the labour'd mole away;
        While self-dependent power can time defy,
430 As rocks resist the billows and the sky.

418 *Torno:* there is a mountain of this name near Lake Como, N. Italy; but the antithesis in ll. 419-20 suggests that Goldsmith meant the River Torne or Tornio, which flows through the mountains of N. Sweden into the Gulf of Bothnia.   *Pambamarca:* a mountain near Quito, Ecuador.
  419 *equinoctial fervours:* the intense heat at the Equator.
  427-30 These lines, according to Boswell, were contributed by Johnson.
  428 *mole:* stone breakwater.

Epitaph on Thomas Parnell

GOLDSMITH'S *Life of Thomas Parnell* appeared in 1770, and this epitaph was probably written in or about that year; it was published in 1776, together with *The Haunch of Venison*. Parnell (1679-1718) was a fellow-Irishman, a minor Augustan poet, and a friend of Swift and Pope.

    This tomb, inscrib'd to gentle PARNEL's name,
    May speak our gratitude, but not his fame.
    What heart but feels his sweetly-moral lay,
    That leads to Truth thro' Pleasure's flow'ry way?
5 Celestial themes confess'd his tuneful aid;
    And Heav'n, that lent him Genius, was repaid.
    Needless to him the tribute we bestow,
    The transitory breath of Fame below:
    More lasting rapture from his Works shall rise,
10 While Converts thank their Poet in the skies.

Song

JAMES BOSWELL published this song in *The London Magazine*, June 1774, explaining that it was originally in the text of *She Stoops to Conquer*, but that Goldsmith omitted it, "as Mrs. *Bulkeley* who played the part [of Kate Hardcastle] did not sing. He sung it himself in private companies very agreeably. The tune is a pretty Irish air, called *The Humours of Balamagairy*. . . ."

    Ah me! when shall I marry me?
        Lovers are plenty; but fail to relieve me.
    He, fond youth, that could carry me,
        Offers to love, but means to deceive me.

3 *carry me:* win me, gain my affections.

*

5   But I will rally and combat the ruiner:
        Not a look, not a smile, shall my passion discover.
    She that gives all to the false one pursuing her,
        Makes but a penitent, loses a lover.

Epilogue to She Stoops To Conquer

THE comedy was first performed on March 15, 1773, and published eleven days later. The Epilogue (Goldsmith called it a "very mawkish thing") was completed only at the last moment, after two other versions had been turned down. It is spoken by Kate Hardcastle, Marlow's intended wife, whom he has mistaken for a captivating bar-maid.

    Well, having stoop'd to conquer with success,
    And gain'd a husband without aid from dress,
    Still as a Bar-maid, I could wish it too,
    As I have conquer'd him to conquer you:
5   And let me say, for all your resolution,
    That pretty Bar-maids have done execution.
    Our life is all a play, compos'd to please,
    "We have our exits and our entrances."
    The first act shews the simple country maid,
10 Harmless and young, of ev'ry thing afraid;
    Blushes when hir'd, and with unmeaning action,
    I hopes as how to give you satisfaction.
    Her second act displays a livelier scene,—
    Th' unblushing Bar-maid of a country inn;
15 Who whisks about the house, at market caters,
    Talks loud, coquets the guests, and scolds the waiters.
    Next the scene shifts to town, and there she soars,
    The chop-house toast of ogling connoisseurs.

8 Quoted from Jaques's famous speech on the seven ages of man, *As You Like It*, II, vii.

11 *unmeaning action:* she is unaware of the way her words (in l. 12) might be taken, and accompanies them with an innocent gesture.

18 *chop-house:* a cheap eating-house in the City of London.

On 'Squires and Cits she there displays her arts,
20 And on the gridiron broils her lovers' hearts—
And as she smiles, her triumphs to compleat,
Even Common Councilmen forget to eat.
The fourth act shews her wedded to the 'Squire,
And Madam now begins to hold it higher;
25 Pretends to taste, at Operas cries *caro*,
And quits her Nancy Dawson, for *Che Faro*.
Doats upon dancing, and in all her pride,
Swims round the room, the *Heinel* of Cheapside:
Ogles and leers with artificial skill,
30 Till having lost in age the power to kill,
She sits all night at cards, and ogles at spadille.
Such, thro' our lives, the eventful history—
The fifth and last act still remains for me.
The Bar-maid now for your protection prays,
35 Turns Female Barrister, and pleads for Bayes.

19 The term *cit* (abbreviation of *citizen*) was applied contemptuously to townsmen in general, shopkeepers and traders in particular.

22 *Common Councilmen:* members of the London City Council.

25 *Pretends to taste:* has pretensions to good taste.   *caro:* Italian for "dear", "fine"; it was a fashionable cry of approval.

26 *Nancy Dawson:* a lively popular song.   *Che Faro:* a famous aria in Gluck's opera *Orfeo* (1762).

28 *Heinel:* Anna Frederica Heinel, a European dancer, enjoying great success in London at this time.   *Cheapside:* an important street in the heart of the commercial (and unfashionable) City of London.

31 *spadille:* the ace of spades, the first trump in the games of ombre and quadrille.

35 *Bayes:* Goldsmith with mock modesty assumes the name of the dramatist ridiculed in the Duke of Buckingham's play, *The Rehearsal* (1672).

Epitaph on Edward Purdon

GOLDSMITH knew Purdon as an undergraduate in Dublin, and later as a hack-writer for London publishers; he died in April 1767. The epitaph appeared anonymously in *The Weekly Magazine, or Edinburgh Amusement* for August 12, 1773, and was first printed as Goldsmith's in 1777. It has two possible "sources": a French quatrain ("La Mort du Sieur Etienne"), and Pope's mock-epitaph on the poet Gay.

> Here lies poor Ned Purdon, from misery freed,
> Who long was a bookseller's hack;
> He led such a damnable life in this world,
> I don't think he'll ever come back.

4 The 1777 text misses the slyness here by reading:
> I don't think, he'll wish to come back.

Retaliation

TOWARDS the end of his life Goldsmith belonged to a convivial group which met informally in the St. James's Coffee House, London. At one of their meetings (probably early 1774) the members produced mock epitaphs on Goldsmith, of which only Garrick's has survived complete:

> Here lies Nolly *Goldsmith*, for shortness call'd Noll,
> Who wrote like an Angel, but talk'd like poor Poll.

(In Garrick's version of the incident, Goldsmith suggested that the two should compose extempore epitaphs on each other, and was baffled when Garrick almost immediately recited his couplet.) Goldsmith set to work to retaliate in a whole series of epitaphs, and was still engaged on the poem when he died, April 4, 1774: it appeared in print fifteen days later.

The poem was hurried through the press, its many errors being put right in the second and third editions, later in 1774. I have accepted all the readings of these two editions which seem to be genuine corrections.

The club members memorialised in the poem are the Dean of Derry, Dr. Thomas Barnard; Edmund Burke, author and statesman; William

Burke, M.P., an intimate friend of Edmund's; Richard Burke, Edmund's younger brother; Richard Cumberland, dramatist; Dr. John Douglas, canon of Windsor; David Garrick, the actor and theatre-manager; John Ridge and Joseph Hickey, Irish lawyers, and Sir Joshua Reynolds, the famous painter.

> Of old, when Scarron his companions invited,
> Each guest brought his dish, and the feast was united;
> If our landlord supplies us with beef, and with fish,
> Let each guest bring himself, and he brings the best dish:
> 5 Our Dean shall be venison, just fresh from the plains;
> Our Burke shall be tongue, with a garnish of brains;
> Our Will shall be wild fowl, of excellent flavour,
> And Dick with his pepper, shall heighten their savour:
> Our Cumberland's sweet-bread, its place shall obtain,
> 10 And Douglas's pudding, substantial and plain:
> Our Garrick's a sallad, for in him we see
> Oil, vinegar, sugar, and saltness agree:
> To make out the dinner, full certain I am,
> That Ridge is anchovy, and Reynolds is lamb;
> 15 That Hickey's a capon, and by the same rule,
> Magnanimous Goldsmith, a goosberry fool:
> At a dinner so various, at such a repast,
> Who'd not be a glutton, and stick to the last:
> Here, waiter, more wine, let me sit while I'm able,
> 20 'Till all my companions sink under the table;
> Then with chaos and blunders encircling my head,
> Let me ponder, and tell what I think of the dead.
>
> Here lies the good Dean, re-united to earth,
> Who mixt reason with pleasure, and wisdom with mirth:
> 25 If he had any faults, he has left us in doubt,
> At least, in six weeks, I could not find 'em out;
> Yet some have declar'd, and it can't be denied 'em,
> That sly-boots was cursedly cunning to hide 'em.

1 *Scarron:* seventeenth-century French dramatist and burlesque poet. In the last months of his life Goldsmith was working on a translation of his *Roman Comique*.

6 *Our Burke shall be tongue:* a tribute to Burke's great powers of oratory.

>   Here lies our good Edmund, whose genius was such,
> 30 We scarcely can praise it, or blame it too much;
>   Who, born for the Universe, narrow'd his mind,
>   And to party gave up, what was meant for mankind.
>   Tho' fraught with all learning, yet straining his throat,
>   To persuade Tommy Townsend to lend him a vote;
> 35 Who, too deep for his hearers, still went on refining,
>   And thought of convincing, while they thought of dining;
>   Tho' equal to all things, for all things unfit,
>   Too nice for a statesman, too proud for a wit:
>   For a patriot too cool; for a drudge, disobedient,
> 40 And too fond of the *right* to pursue the *expedient*.
>   In short, 'twas his fate, unemploy'd, or in place, Sir,
>   To eat mutton cold, and cut blocks with a razor.
>
>   Here lies honest William, whose heart was a mint,
>   While the owner ne'er knew half the good that was in't;
> 45 The pupil of impulse, it forc'd him along,
>   His conduct still right, with his argument wrong;
>   Still aiming at honour, yet fearing to roam,
>   The coachman was tipsy, the chariot drove home;
>   Would you ask for his merits, alas! he had none,
> 50 What was good was spontaneous, his faults were his own.
>
>   Here lies honest Richard, whose fate I must sigh at,
>   Alas, that such frolic should now be so quiet!
>   What spirits were his, what wit and what whim,
>   Now breaking a jest, and now breaking a limb;

31-2 To some of his friends Burke's entry into politics (he was elected M.P. 1765) seemed a sad waste of his manifold talents.

34 *Townsend:* Thomas Townsend, M.P. and later Viscount Sydney. Boswell believed that Townsend's adverse comments in Parliament on Dr. Johnson's pension had earned him Goldsmith's sneers. Cf. also l. 88.

38 *nice:* scrupulous, punctilious.

39 *patriot:* See p. 112, Epilogue to *The Sister*, l. 16, note.

42 Alluding to Burke's financial difficulties, and (as Goldsmith saw it) his intellectual brilliance quite wasted on stupid politicians.

55 Now wrangling and grumbling to keep up the ball,
    Now teazing and vexing, yet laughing at all?
    In short so provoking a Devil was Dick,
    That we wish'd him full ten times a day at Old Nick.
    But missing his mirth and agreeable vein,
60 As often we wish'd to have Dick back again.

    Here Cumberland lies having acted his parts,
    The Terence of England, the mender of hearts;
    A flattering painter, who made it his care
    To draw men as they ought to be, not as they are.
65 His gallants are all faultless, his women divine,
    And comedy wonders at being so fine;
    Like a tragedy queen he has dizen'd her out,
    Or rather like tragedy giving a rout.
    His fools have their follies so lost in a croud
70 Of virtues and feelings, that folly grows proud,
    And coxcombs, alike in their failings alone,
    Adopting his portraits are pleas'd with their own.
    Say, where has our poet this malady caught,
    Or wherefore his characters thus without fault?
75 Say was it that vainly directing his view,
    To find out men's virtues and finding them few,
    Quite sick of pursuing each troublesome elf,
    He grew lazy at last and drew from himself?

55 *keep up the ball:* keep the conversation from flagging.

66 Cumberland wrote "sentimental comedies" full of virtuous characters with fine feelings (hence *sweet-bread*, l. 9). In an essay on "Laughing and Sentimental Comedy" Goldsmith calls the latter a "species of bastard tragedy" that is driving true humour from the stage: he notes that among classical writers Terence came nearest to this mingling of comic and tragic. Goldsmith's own comedies are of the robuster "laughing" kind.

67 *dizen'd out:* decked out, dressed in finery. Cf. Swift, "The Grand Question Debated", l. 102: "For sure, I had *dizen'd* you out like a Queen."

68 *rout:* a reception or large party.

Here Douglas retires from his toils to relax,
80 The scourge of impostors, the terror of quacks:
Come all ye quack bards, and ye quacking divines,
Come and dance on the spot where your tyrant reclines;
When Satire and Censure encircl'd his throne,
I fear'd for your safety, I fear'd for my own;
85 But now he is gone, and we want a detector,
Our Dodds shall be pious, our Kenricks shall lecture;
Macpherson write bombast, and call it a style,
Our Townshend make speeches, and I shall compile;
New Lauders and Bowers the Tweed shall cross over,
90 No countryman living their tricks to discover;
Detection her taper shall quench to a spark,
And Scotchman meet Scotchman and cheat in the dark.

Here lies David Garrick, describe me who can,
An abridgment of all that was pleasant in man;
95 As an actor, confest without rival to shine,
As a wit, if not first, in the very first line,
Yet with talents like these, and an excellent heart,
The man had his failings, a dupe to his art;

80 Douglas had exposed the literary impositions and forgeries of two fellow Scotsmen, Archibald Bower and William Lauder (ll. 89-90).

86 The Reverend Dr. William Dodd was a fashionable, vain, loose-living clergyman (he was later hanged for forgery). Dr. William Kenrick had begun in January 1774 a series of public lectures on "The School of Shakespeare". He had written hostile reviews of several of Goldsmith's works, and was probably responsible for a particularly offensive open letter to Goldsmith in *The London Packet*, March 24, 1773.

87 James *Macpherson*, best-known for his "translations" of Gaelic epics (largely of his own invention), had published in 1773 a rendering of Homer's *Iliad* into English prose. His style is ludicrously abrupt and emphatic, though Macpherson claimed in his Preface to have "studied simplicity of expression and smoothness of language".

88 *compile:* several of Goldsmith's prose-works (e.g. *The Roman History*, 1769; *History of England from the Earliest Times*, 1771) were pot-boilers unashamedly compiled from various authorities. At the time of *Retaliation* he was "compiling" a *Grecian History*, published posthumously 1774.

Like an ill-judging beauty, his colours he spread,
100 And beplaister'd, with rouge, his own natural red.
On the stage he was natural, simple, affecting,
'Twas only that, when he was off, he was acting:
With no reason on earth to go out of his way,
He turn'd and he varied full ten times a day;
105 Tho' secure of our hearts, yet confoundedly sick,
If they were not his own by finessing and trick;
He cast off his friends, as a huntsman his pack;
For he knew when he pleased he could whistle them back.
Of praise a mere glutton, he swallowed what came,
110 And the puff of a dunce, he mistook it for fame;
'Till his relish grown callous, almost to disease,
Who pepper'd the highest, was surest to please.
But let us be candid, and speak out our mind,
If dunces applauded, he paid them in kind.
115 Ye Kenricks, ye Kellys, and Woodfalls so grave,
What a commerce was yours, while you got and you gave?
How did Grub-street re-echo the shouts that you rais'd,
While he was beroscius'd, and you were beprais'd?
But peace to his spirit, wherever it flies,
120 To act as an angel, and mix with the skies:
Those poets, who owe their best fame to his skill,
Shall still be his flatterers, go where he will.

106 *finessing:* in the game of whist, attempting to take a trick by bluffing.

110 *puff:* extravagant praise—by theatre critics and reviewers.

115 For *KENRICK* see note to l. 86. Hugh *KELLY*, author of sentimental comedies, enjoyed Garrick's favour; production of his *False Delicacy* delayed the first performance of Goldsmith's *Good Natur'd Man*. William *Woodfall* was an editor and theatre critic; his hostile review of *She Stoops to Conquer* included a defence of Sentimental Comedy.

117 *Grub-street:* a London street inhabited during the eighteenth century by hack-writers.

118 *beroscius'd:* The critics acclaimed Garrick as a second *Roscius*, who was the most celebrated actor in classical Rome, and came to be regarded as the ideal actor.

Old Shakespeare, receive him, with praise and with love,
And Beaumonts and Bens be his Kellys above.

125   Here Hickey reclines, a most blunt, pleasant creature,
And slander itself must allow him good-nature:
He cherish'd his friend, and he relish'd a bumper;
Yet one fault he had, and that one was a thumper:
Perhaps you may ask if the man was a miser?
130 I answer, no, no, for he always was wiser;
Too courteous, perhaps, or obligingly flat;
His very worst foe can't accuse him of that.
Perhaps he confided in men as they go,
And so was too foolishly honest; ah, no.
135 Then what was his failing? come tell it, and burn ye;
He was, could he help it? a special attorney.
     Here Reynolds is laid, and to tell you my mind,
He has not left a better or wiser behind;
His pencil was striking, resistless and grand,
140 His manners were gentle, complying and bland;
Still born to improve us in every part,
His pencil our faces, his manners our heart:
To coxcombs averse, yet most civilly steering,
When they judged without skill he was still hard of hearing:
145 When they talk'd of their Raphaels, Corregios and stuff,
He shifted his trumpet, and only took snuff.

124 The Jacobean dramatists Francis Beaumont and Ben Jonson.
127 *bumper:* a glass filled to the brim, especially for a toast.
131 *flat:* insipid, lacking spirit: i.e., too deferential, too ready to oblige.
135 *burn ye:* a milder form of "Be damned to you!" A note in the first two editions quaintly describes it as "a familiar method of salutation in Ireland amongst the lower classes of the people".
136 *special attorney:* a lawyer empowered to act in a specific case or a particular court (in contrast to Attorney-General).
139 *pencil:* the painter's brush, or (figuratively) his art.
144 Reynolds was very deaf, and used an ear-trumpet.
145 Raphael and Correggio were two of the most famous Italian painters of the Renaissance.
146 Reynolds was an inveterate snuff-taker. But *to take snuff* could also

mean "to be offended": Reynolds tried to avoid listening to conceited people showing off their knowledge of art, and hid his irritation in a pinch of snuff.

After l. 146 the fifth edition (also 1774) added a rather undistinguished epitaph on Caleb Whitefoord, wine-merchant and wit. It was claimed that Goldsmith had handed the lines to a friend a few days before his death; quite possibly Whitefoord wrote them himself. The poem is certainly unfinished, but what we lack, according to the list of guests in the opening lines, is not Whitefoord's epitaph, but those of Ridge and, perhaps, of Goldsmith himself.

Appendix A

The Traveller, ll. 381 ff.

GOLDSMITH sketched out this political doctrine in an essay, "The Revolution in Low Life", printed two years before *The Traveller*; and two years after the poem appeared he set it out more systematically in a long harangue by Dr. Primrose, the Vicar of Wakefield. Some of Goldsmith's editors have declared the transitions in this part of *The Traveller*, particularly ll. 393-4, rather awkward; I give here a summary of the doctrine, based on ch. xix of *The Vicar of Wakefield*, which may help to clarify the poem's more passionate and less firmly articulated argument.

1. Mankind naturally hates tyranny, and seeks to reduce the number of petty tyrants by electing a monarch.
2. These petty tyrants (the "contending chiefs" of l. 381), repining under their Sovereign, attempt to undermine the monarchy and limit its scope.
3. They acquire power by acquiring wealth—the more easily in a commercial nation, since only those already rich can prosecute, and profit from, trade. Hence "wealth, in all commercial states, is found to accumulate, and all such have hitherto in time become aristocratical".
4. The rich buy the dependence of the poor: in the poem they not only "purchase slaves at home" (l. 388) but also, as in *The Deserted Village*, dispossess the cottagers (ll. 401 ff.).
5. So the task of preserving freedom falls to those of the middle rank. And the fate of England, should this middle rank be overwhelmed, "may be seen by turning our eyes to Holland, Genoa, or Venice, where the laws govern the poor, and the rich govern the law".
6. If the middle rank feels itself inadequate to this task it must concentrate its efforts on upholding the monarch, "for he divides the power of the rich, and calls off the great from falling with tenfold weight on the middle order placed beneath them" (cf. especially l. 376). The monarch is sacred, "and every diminution of his power in war, or in peace, is an infringement upon the real liberties of the subject".

Appendix B

The Deserted Village, ll. 43-6

GOLDSMITH's account of the bittern in his *History of the Earth, and Animated Nature* (published posthumously, London, 1774) is worth quoting for its own sake, revealing as it does his sensitiveness to sounds and his accuracy of description, as well as for the light it throws on *The Deserted Village*.

Of the Bittern or Mire-drum

Those who have walked in an evening by the sedgy sides of unfrequented rivers, must remember a variety of notes from different water-fowl: the loud scream of the wild goose, the croaking of the mallard, the whining of the lapwing, and the tremulous neighing of the jack-snipe. But of all those sounds, there is none so dismally hollow as the booming of the bittern. It is impossible for words to give those who have not heard this evening-call an adequate idea of its solemnity. It is like the interrupted bellowing of a bull, but hollower and louder, and is heard at a mile's distance, as if issuing from some formidable being that resided at the bottom of the waters. . . .

I remember in the place where I was a boy with what terror this bird's note affected the whole village; they considered it as the presage of some sad event; and generally found or made one to succeed it.

(vol. VI, pp. 1-2, 4)

Writing in a later chapter of the lapwing and other "Small Birds of the Crane Kind", Goldsmith observes that they "chiefly chuse to breed in . . . some island surrounded with sedgy moors, where men seldom resort" (vol. VI, p. 32). It is important for the poem's purposes that both the bittern and the lapwing prefer solitude. Their presence emphasises for us the surrounding desolation, and the phrase "solitary guest" (l. 43) is a poignant reminder of vanished hospitality and good-fellowship.

Select Bibliography

I Editions

The Works of Oliver Goldsmith, edited by Arthur Friedman, will be published shortly by the Clarendon Press; this will be the definitive edition. Two very full selections have been made by Richard Garnett (*Goldsmith: Selected Works*, London, 1950) and by F. W. Hilles (*The Vicar of Wakefield and Other Writings*, New York, 1955). *The Complete Poetical Works* were edited by Austin Dobson (Oxford, 1906), with copious annotation.

An important addition to the canon was made in 1927 by R. S. Crane, with his *New Essays by Oliver Goldsmith* (Chicago), though the authenticity of some of the eighteen essays he printed has since been questioned. Miss K. C. Balderston has edited the *Collected Letters* (Cambridge, 1928); there are, unfortunately, very few of them.

A Prospect of Society, the first version of *The Traveller*, is available in an edition by W. B. Todd (Charlottesville, 1956).

II Biographies

Boswell's *Life of Johnson* and *London Journal* contain indispensable material, though he is clearly a prejudiced witness. A more sympathetic and equally lively memoir by Reynolds, Goldsmith's most intimate friend, is included in *Portraits by Sir Joshua Reynolds*, edited by F. W. Hilles (New York and London, 1952); Hilles's Introduction is specially good on Goldsmith's often misunderstood style of conversation.

The definitive biography is R. M. Wardle's *Oliver Goldsmith* (Lawrence [Kansas] and London, 1957).

III Studies

Two short but useful accounts of Goldsmith's writings are the chapter by Boris Ford in *The Pelican Guide to English Literature* (ed. B. Ford), vol. IV, "From Dryden to Johnson" (1957); and the booklet on Goldsmith by A. N. Jeffares in the "Writers and Their Work" series (London, 1957).

Donald Davie's *Purity of Diction in English Verse* (London, 1952) has some helpful comments on Goldsmith's poetry, and his edition of eighteenth-century poems (*The Late Augustans*, London, 1958) has useful background material in its Introduction, and an excellent brief note on *The Deserted*

Village on p. 118. Two important articles on this poem are H. J. Bell's "*The Deserted Village* and Goldsmith's Social Doctrines" (*Publications of the Modern Language Association of America*, vol. LIX [1944], pp. 747-72), and Earl Miner's "The Making of *The Deserted Village*" (*Huntington Library Quarterly*, vol. XXII [1959], pp. 125-41). Kenneth MacLean's *Agrarian Age: A Background for Wordsworth* (New Haven and London, 1950) surveys agricultural developments, enclosures, etc., in late eighteenth-century England, and sets *The Deserted Village* in this agrarian context (pp. 30 ff.).

Goldsmith's writings are remarkably homogeneous, and one work will often illuminate another. The third and fourth chapters of MacDonald Emslie's *Goldsmith: The Vicar of Wakefield* (Studies in English Literature series, London, 1963) are very relevant to *The Traveller* and *The Deserted Village*.